Want a good decision?

Find a good frame.

FRAME *SHIFT*

The Key to Better Decisions

Lynn B. Davidson

Library of Congress Cataloging-in-Publication Data

Davidson, Lynn B.
    Frame Shift: The Key to Better Decisions/ Lynn Davidson—1st Ed.
    Includes bibliographical references.

    ISBN 978-1-98339-227-6
    1. Better decisions, 2. Decision traps, 3. Decision frames

To Jamie, Joey, Rory, and Finn,
with love and hope

CONTENTS

PREFACE

The ideas behind this book began many years ago in the Libyan Desert. There, among the dunes and wadis and brilliant sky, I witnessed a bad decision. As an engineer trained in how to extract oil from underground reservoirs, I knew the right and wrong ways to do it. Do it right, you might get as much as 30 percent of the oil in the ground. Do it wrong, get less than half that amount, a huge lost opportunity. One of our competitors was doing it wrong.

Because I was fresh out of college and lacked experience, I assumed that my conclusion was wrong, that I had missed something. Eventually I concluded I had been right. That was a puzzle. How could well trained engineers and managers make such a bad decision?

As I learned more about decision making, it became clear how they made the bad decision: they made an error right at the start. That's the biggest source of error in many decisions, the start. The way a decision is framed at the start strongly determines whether the outcome will be a good or bad decision. The competitors in Libya had used a bad decision frame.

As time went on, I came to learn that my Libyan conclusion was broadly applicable to any decision. Choose a good frame and you increase greatly your chances of a good decision. Frame poorly and the decision will probably be bad. This book has been written to explore in detail this key idea.

In what follows, you will learn the key role frames play in making decisions, and you will learn five key skills to enable you to frame your decisions well.

When you read this book you take a step on a journey to improve *your* decisions. This journey has no final destination, only better and better decisions. Along the way you will gain insight into how your prior decisions have been hampered, why others sometimes make poor decisions, and how you can improve your chances of avoiding poor decisions in the future.

ACKNOWLEDGMENTS

Many people have written extensively about decision making and ways to improve it. Their ideas have strongly influenced the content of this book. In particular, I am indebted to Russell Ackoff, Edward deBono, Daniel Kahneman, Ralph Keeney, Gary Klein, Amos Tversky, Howard Raiffa, J. Edward Russo, Thomas Saaty, Paul J. H. Schoemaker, and Roger von Oech.

Most notably, the writings of Drs. Russo and choemaker increased greatly my appreciation for the role of decision frames and inspired me to look into the concept more closely.

To Eleanor Corcoran belongs the credit for mproving the clarity and consistency of this book. She has strengthened significantly the ideas presented and greatly improved the clarity and conciseness of the writing.

This book also owes a great deal to my clients, who willingly took me into their confidence on decisions they were making and allowed me to work with them on those decisions. The experience gained from this work has strengthened greatly the ideas you will soon discover.

1

THE RAREST GIFT

*The rarest gift that God bestows on man
is the capacity for decision.*

Dean Acheson

A powerful idea can be so simple that its value is overlooked. The concept of mental frames is such an idea. Mental frames are the boundaries around our window to the world. Without mental frames we would drown in a torrent of input, inundated by the incessant, rapidly changing, cacophonous, chaotic information that bombards us. A frame acts as a filter. It limits our perception to only a restricted, manageable portion of reality.

A simple illustration: Look around you. Look carefully and honestly for red objects, and only red objects. Then close your eyes. Recall, with your eyes closed, everything that is … green. Not red, but green. Try it. What happened? Did you find red objects easy to recall, but green hard to recall? As you frame for red, you tend not to notice other colors. They are, in effect, hidden.

Frames enable us to function, but they have an obvious price: we tend to be blind to what they exclude.

Our focus will be on frames related to decisions. Whenever you make a decision, you first set a frame. The frame is how you characterize the decision. Like all mental frames, it exposes certain things but hides others. This is why the frame choice determines whether you make a good or bad decision.

We'll now look more closely at decision frames, then examine how they affect decision quality.

To begin, consider how frame choice shapes a decision about dinner. Suppose you frame the dinner decision as "What shall we have for dinner?" Notice what you think about (and don't think about).

Change the frame to "Where shall we go for dinner?" Now attention is on a totally different set of considerations. Each dinner decision creates a different focus, and a different blindness.

The most potent and overlooked attribute of decision frames is this:

You can choose.

You don't need to use the first frame that enters your mind (and one always will). You can choose a better frame if the first one is not good.

Think about a family decision, for example, a decision about the family residence. You are not stuck with the first decision frame that occurs to you. Suppose the frame is "What kind of home do we want?" You are not stuck with this. You could shift to a different frame, such as "Where would we like to live?" Each frame leads to a different focus.

Here's another example to demonstrate that you can choose. Think about the strategy for a business, say a hot dog stand. Suppose you start with a decision frame based on the question, "How can we provide distinctive value to our key customers?" With this frame, you identify key customers, then identify how to meet their top-priority needs with hot dogs and services these customers will love.

Your competition doesn't enter the picture until you start rating your value-creation ideas against competitive offerings to find ideas that are distinctive.

Now consider the hot dog business with a different frame: "How can we take market share away from our competitor, Hot Dog Stand X, and become No. 1 in the area?" Notice how your focus is changed by the new frame. You focus now on Hot Dog Stand X, its strengths and weaknesses. Consideration of customers tends to be neglected, except with regard to their response to your offering vs. that of Stand X. You think about how to pit your strength against X's weaknesses, about feints and signals, about the competitive role of each product.

I am not suggesting whether the first or second hot-dog frame is better. This example simply illustrates that *you can and do* choose the frame by the question you select. And the example shows how your focus shifts when you shift the frame, as does what you pay attention to and what you ignore.

Think about a strategy for any business, framing first for customers, then for competition. Experience how drastically each frame differs in the focus created, opportunities exposed, and risks hidden.

Good Decisions--The Challenge

How much emphasis have you seen on how to make good decisions? How much attention have you paid to how you make your personal decisions or business decisions? How much attention do you pay to the decision process you use, to be sure that the process is a good one?

People want to make good decisions, but too often don't spend the time needed to develop the necessary skills. One reason: they make poor decisions about what is needed to make good decisions.

Another reason: people avoid thinking about how to make better decisions. Such thinking can be confusing, uncomfortable, and disturbing. How even to begin? This reaction is not surprising, particularly if one has never been taught the essential skills and tools.

Many people assume that they should just be able to make decisions--no skill required. This assumption is what leads to the discomfort and confusion. Imagine thinking you could play golf the first time you held a club in your hand. That's what the assumption is like. And it is wrong. There is no skill involved in just making a decision. Tossing a coin or rolling some dice will get the job done. But to make a *good* decision, having the appropriate skills helps greatly.

Mastery of the following five frame skills will put you on track to make better decisions:

- Know your frame--there's more to it than you may think.
- Manage your emotions--they play a central role in good decisions.
- Shift to a good frame when needed--this can be tricky.
- Know how frames are used to persuade and negotiate --frames control the game.
- Avoid frame traps--your mind tricks you in many ways.

We explore these skills in Chapters 2-6. To prepare for those chapters, we will first look more closely at how we make decisions and why the frame is so important.

There is an abundance of information available on decision making and decision analysis.[1] People in many organizations have received training based on this information. This training, however, often does not address decision frames sufficiently and does not expose the debilitating problems bad decision frames cause.

A good discussion of decision frames can be found in two books by J. Edward Russo and Paul J. H. Schoemaker, *Decision Traps* and *Winning Decisions*[2]. Their ideas complement what is provided here. Both books are well worth reading.

Chip and Dan Heath provide another valuable resource related to frames in their 2013 book *Decisive: How to Make Better Choices in Life and Work*.[3] They explore ways to improve identifying possible decision choices, a key step in decision making.

To start our exploration of decision making, let's first look more closely at the importance of decisions for business success, then look at how decisions are made and why the right decision frame is so important.

Decisions and Organization Success

The current situation of any organization -- family, city, church, business, etc. -- is the result of decisions made in the past by the organization's former and current leaders.

The future success of an organization depends on good decisions made now and in the future. A consistent pattern of future good decisions is likely to produce a more successful organization and a greater contribution to society than is a pattern of mediocre decisions.

Some may say unforeseen events beyond our control matter more than the quality of our decisions—luck is more important than good decisions. These statements miss the point. Events, both foreseen and unforeseen, do shape the future. Sometimes we are lucky, sometimes not.

What matters is how we respond to events that do occur, good or bad. If we respond with good decisions, our success will likely be better than if we respond with poor decisions.

The history of General Motors (GM) illustrates these ideas. From the 1920's through the 1960's GM grew to become the icon of American success because of the good decisions of its President and Chairman, Alfred P.

Sloan, Jr. and his team. After Sloan retired in 1956, GM coasted through the 1960's with no major changes in its business model or strategy. Starting in the early 1970's, however, GM's leaders began making too many poor decisions and persisted in so doing for the next forty years (with some notable exceptions, such as the start of Saturn and the introduction of On Star service). GM's June 29, 2014 recall of 7,610,862 automobiles to fix a 10-year-old error shows that the pattern of poor decisions continued at least until the most-recent CEO change.

From the early 1970's through 2009, GM lost market share and experienced poor and declining profitability. At the same time, management increased its level of debt significantly.

GM's almost-final reckoning came when the 2007-8 financial crisis hit.[4] GM's sales plunged and the company could no longer make its loan payments. In June 2009, GM declared bankruptcy. It reemerged from bankruptcy a few months later, thanks to a Federal bailout, but holders of GM stock and bonds lost most of their money and many employees lost their jobs.

Today, GM's new CEO Mary Barra appears to be making good decisions that are improving the company's focus and profitability. It will be interesting to see if she succeeds.

Now let's examine another mother lode of bad decisions and bad results--the 2007 bursting of the housing bubble. Some examples of the bad decisions:

- President Carter's 1977 well-intentioned, but ill-conceived decision to force banks and S&L's to lend to lower-income borrowers through the Community Reinvestment Act;
- President Clinton's 1998 decision to expand Fannie Mae and Freddy Mac's powers so the two government sponsored enterprises could vastly expand their role in home financing;
- Fed Chairman Alan Greenspan's decision to keep interest rates low too long;
- The decisions of many individuals to buy homes they could not afford in the belief that prices would continue to go up;
- The decisions of greedy lenders to lend to unsound borrowers;

- The decisions of banks and pension funds to buy packaged bundles of high-risk home loans, thinking this created diversification when it didn't.

In the 2004-7 period, the dumb housing-related decisions being made were based on three false beliefs:

1. Housing prices would continue to go up.
2. Lending risk was insured.
3. Bundled portfolios of risky mortgages were safe just because credit rating agencies gave them erroneously high ratings.

As with all bubbles, the housing bubble was created by the folly of many. The bubble may have set a modern record for bad decisions. And the bursting of the bubble clearly illustrates that bad decisions lead to bad results.

There were a few good decisions related to the crisis. For example, Fed Chairman Ben Bernanke's actions to increase the money supply quickly in late 2007 and throughout 2008 prevented a more rapid and significant economic collapse. Unfortunately, in this crisis, such good decisions were quite rare, far less frequent than needed for the good of the United States and the world.

Let's now turn away from the recent financial crisis and consider the impact of good and bad decisions at individual businesses.

There appears to be a strong correlation between good performance and good decisions, as well as poor performance and poorer decisions. For example, exceptional growth of companies in slow-growth, highly competitive industries can be attributed to consistently good decisions. Companies like Fastenal in nuts and bolts, Ikea in furniture, Nucor in steel, Progressive in auto insurance, Southwest Airlines, Starbuck's, and Walmart have all grown through good decisions. These companies, and others like them, have had many years of significant revenue and profit growth. They enjoyed these gains while competitors making poorer decisions did not.

Good decisions have driven the success of firms in information technology industries, where rapid, disruptive change is frequent. Companies like Adobe, Amazon, Alphabet, Apple, Autodesk, Cisco, Dell, Facebook, Intel, Microsoft, Netflix, Nvidia, and Oracle are examples.

The history of IBM shows an up and down pattern similar to GM's[5,] but with a better finish. In the 1950's and 60's, IBM was considered the best managed business in the world. It coasted through the 70's with its reputation intact.

But troubles began in 1980. IBM's management boldly predicted sales would double to $100 billion by 1990, driven by increased sales of mainframe computers. At the same time, IBM essentially abandoned the successful personal computer business it had started. The growth projection and abandonment of the PC were based on bad assumptions that ignored the onrushing changes created by ever faster, cheaper, smaller computers.

IBM's executives thought their company needed more large-computer manufacturing capacity to meet its erroneous growth forecast. To fund that capacity, the company broke an implied promise with its customers. Previously, IBM seemed to say "We will take care of your information technology needs." IBM had rented computers to its customers and provided excellent support and maintenance. Now IBM forced its customers to buy the machines they had been renting. It also cut funds for customer support, leading to poorer customer service and less perceived value.

IBM never came close to its $100 billion forecast. It opened new factories, only to close them two years later.

For the first time in its history, the company was forced to lay off workers. IBM almost failed due to bad decisions.

IBM's decline continued until 1993 when Lou Gerstner took over and shifted IBM's decision frame, focus, and business model. Thanks to Gerstner and his team, IBM avoided GM's fate. IBM today has again become and continues to be a successful business.

To see what really bad decisions can do to a business, look at companies like Adelphia, Enron, and Worldcom from the 1990's: wealth decimated, executives in jail, and the draconian burden of Sarbanes-Oxley compliance for all other U.S. public companies. More recently, investors lost billions in Theranos. They were taken in by bogus claims about the reliability of Theranos' blood-test machine, Edison, which is basically useless.

The business examples just discussed illustrate the key point: decision quality matters. Good decisions are more likely to produce better results for you than bad ones. Therefore, if you want better results, pay attention to how you make your decisions.

The Key to Good Decisions

How can you make good decisions and avoid bad ones? As previously noted, choose a good decision frame at the start. Nothing else affects the quality of a decision more.

To understand why the start is so crucial we need to look more closely at decisions: how they arise, what we mean by good ones, and how we make them. With this information, you will be able to understand more clearly why the starting point is so important in determining decision quality.

When Is a Decision Needed?

You sense the need to make a decision when you perceive a gap between the current state of things and the conditions you desire.[6] Think about it. If things are going along fine and you anticipate they will continue to do so, you don't feel the need to make a decision. But get a pang of hunger and you feel the need to make a decision. Encounter a period of poor growth in your business, and you will sense the need to make decisions about improved growth.

Throughout each day, you make many decisions. Each is triggered by a perceived gap. Most are minor decisions often made without deliberate thought in reaction to minor gaps. The traffic is too slow, so how to find a faster route? The music on the radio is not what you want, so you change the station or turn off the radio. Your daughter is having trouble at school, so how do you fix the situation?

A few decisions will be more significant: Our sales of product X are below our expectations. Should we take corrective action, and if so, what?

Without a perceived current or future gap, the need to make a decision simply does not arise. It should be noted this can be dangerous if we fail to perceive a gap when there is one. In such cases you could fail to make a decision and experience unfortunate consequences.

It is equally true that you can think you need to make a decision when none is required. This will happen when you perceive what you think is a gap, but it is really a mirage.

What is a Good Decision?

You have made a good decision if you have selected and effectively implemented the best choice among the options available for moving from the current situation to a preferred situation. The best choice will be the one with the highest chance of closing the gap between the current and desired state.

In 1906, Henry Ford perceived a gap[7]: he wanted to provide a car everyone could afford at a time when only high-income people could afford one.

The gap between where Ford was and where he wanted to be led him to a decision frame focused on how to achieve cost-efficient manufacturing. This frame led to his choice of providing low-cost autos through assembly-line methods as the best choice among many possibilities.

His choice fit the market situation. He had the necessary resources and capabilities to implement the choice successfully. The level of risk was acceptable. And he implemented his choice effectively. That's a good decision. It led to a car many could afford and led to his dominance of the auto industry for 20 years.

Ford's leadership ended in the 1920's when Alfred Sloan, the CEO at General Motors, used a different frame to make a good decision: give the public a range of choices, each appealing to a different income level, based on price and quality.
Henry Ford responded with a bad decision: stick with a single car model. By 1931, GM had surpassed Ford to become the top U.S. auto company.

How Do You Make a Decision?

Evidence indicates you make decisions in one of two ways: pattern matching[8] or analysis. With pattern matching, you compare the decision situation to similar situations in the past. You make a choice of action based on what worked best in those previous, similar situations.

Pattern matching produces very fast decisions and if the decision maker is experienced, the decisions are often quite good. This decision making approach is commonly used for many everyday decisions and for many rapid-response situations, such as police, fire, military, and medical emergency actions. It is also the approach bred into us from our primitive origins.

The approach does not work if the decision maker is inexperienced or unknowingly chooses a prior experience that differs in some critical way from the current situation.

My wife and I had an emergency-room encounter that illustrates the risk. A cat had scratched her ear. As we were attending a performance of *Les Misérables* that evening, her ear got redder and hotter. We went to an emergency room nearby. The first doctor to examine her lacked sufficient experience for accurate pattern matching and misdiagnosed the infection as viral. Fortunately, a second, more experienced, doctor came along and correctly diagnosed the condition as a rapidly spreading bacterial infection requiring immediate treatment. If the second doctor had not come along, it's possible my wife would no longer be with me.

Pattern matching can be done in a mindless sort of way. Robert Cialdini provides entertaining examples of this. He calls them fixed action patterns.[9] An individual "decides" on a course of action due to a trigger event. But the decision is made without conscious thought. He calls this the click- whirr pattern: the trigger event clicks in a preprogrammed mental "tape" that whirrs into action.

He cites the example of how the "cheep cheep" sound of turkey chicks causes female turkeys to behave maternally toward the chicks. That's reasonable, but the female turkeys will mother *anything* that emits the "cheap cheap" sound! Even its traditional nemesis, a bobcat, will be mothered.

In another example of click-whirr, he describes an experiment by Ellen Langer in which a person tries to jump a line in making copies at a Xerox machine. The person says "Excuse me. I have 5 pages. May I use the Xerox machine?" Sixty percent of the time, the person is able to jump the line. Pretty good. But in other tests the line jumper adds an additional phrase, saying "Excuse me. I have 5 pages. May I use the Xerox machine *because I have some copies to make.*" With the added phrase, the success rate is 93 percent! The word "because" creates a click-whirr response leading to almost total mindless compliance with the line-jumping request.

Many decisions are made using pattern matching, both in mindful and mindless ways. But most more-important decisions are made using an approach the decision makers hopes is more rational and analytical.

The analytical decision-making approach can be described as a six-step process:

1. Choose the frame for the decision.

2. Analyze the situation (which may lead to a change in the decision frame).

3. Identify choices.

4. Evaluate choices.

5. Select a preferred choice.

6. Implement the preferred choice.

Listing the steps in this manner may seem to imply a lengthy deliberative process. Actually, for most decisions, the minor, every day decisions, if you use the analytical approach, you do so rapidly and without much thought.

For example, the frame "How shall I get to work?" is usually followed almost instantly by consideration and evaluation of choices, resulting in a choice of commuting method and route. The evaluation of routes may or may not be aided by route-planning apps. Total time spent-- mere seconds. All this is done intuitively, with some pattern matching and little conscious thought.

Listing the six decision-making steps may seem to imply they are done sequentially. The reality is usually different. There can be considerable bouncing back and forth between the steps. For example, thinking about choices may lead to a change in the decision frame. Evaluating a choice may stimulate identification of new choices. And so on.

The six-step sequence is the commonly recommended way to make decisions and it provides a useful framework for communicating the activities involved in making a decision.

It will help for us to look at each of the six steps more closely.

1. Choose the Frame

The frame is our description of a decision and the situation related to it. As noted previously, in making a decision, you always choose a frame first. You cannot make a decision without doing so.

The frame is a simplified version of reality. As noted earlier, the simplification enables you to make the decision by excluding a vast amount of information considered unimportant. And that simplification has a price: you can overlook something important that could lead to a better decision.

The frame has four parts:

1. The perceived gap
2. The framing question
3. Frame-related assumptions
4. Decision success measures.

The perceived gap is your perception of a difference between where you are and where you want to be. As noted earlier, the perceived gap is the trigger for a decision aimed at closing the gap.

The second component of the frame is the framing question. It sets the focus for a decision. For example, the framing question "Where shall we go on vacation?" focuses attention in a different direction than the framing question, "What shall we do on our vacation?" The first question leads to a search for places to go. The second focuses your attention in an entirely different direction, on activities.

Notice that once you have chosen a framing question such as "Where shall we go on vacation?" you identify success measures with which you will judge possible destination choices and, later, judge how good a decision you made. These success measures are the third component of the frame. The success measures may change when you change the framing question.

Assumptions are the fourth component of a decision frame. Assumptions lead you to the perception that there is a gap. Assumptions about how to describe the decision lead you to the framing question. And assumptions about what constitutes success lead you to success measures.

With any decision, you make some assumptions with full awareness of doing so. But often you also make many assumptions of which you are not aware.

Once you have chosen a framing question like "where to go on vacation", the question highlights still more assumptions related to the question. For the "where to go on vacation" question some of these assumptions will relate to how much different destinations will cost, how much you can afford, what types of destinations to consider, how the date of the vacation affects your choice, and so on.

For the vacation decision, with the "where to go" framing question, you concentrate on assumptions that relate to places to go. Information not related to those assumptions tends to be ignored.

Now imagine deciding on a vacation using the second framing question, "What shall we do on our vacation?"

What assumptions do you make? They focus more on suitable types of activities, where the activities can be done, what they will cost, and so on.

Many of these assumptions can be quite different from those from the first framing question. The "what to do" question highlights issues and considerations minimized or ignored with "where to go" question. Consideration of where to go becomes secondary to the consideration of activities.

The two questions thus point in different directions, and, as Exhibit 1.1 suggests, they can lead to different decisions.

Exhibit 1.1 – Different Frames, Different Decisions

Of course, the one framing question does not preclude the other. You could decide first on a desired activity and then on a destination. Or make the two decisions in the opposite order: destination, then activity. Notice that

Activity ➔ Destination

will usually give you choices that differ from

Destination ➔ Activity.

This is because the first decision constrains the second.

In the activity first -- destination second sequence, your activity choice shapes the frame for your destination choice:

if you want to play golf, you will consider only destinations with golf. If in the Destination ➔Activity sequence, the choice of Dallas, Texas is made, this choice will restrict the activity frame to what is available in Dallas. Mountain climbing, for example, is out since Dallas has no mountains (unless you want to climb high-rise office buildings).

Decisions in business are often linked. Initial decisions are therefore particularly important because they shape the frames and restrict the focus of later ones, for good or ill. This is one reason why good product-development processes emphasize heavy senior management involvement at the start of a project. Good decision frames and good decisions at the start can avoid expensive disasters later, when fixing things is much more difficult.

Many decisions are path dependent. In such cases, once a first decision is made, it establishes consequences that are very hard to reverse and leads to additional decisions that arise only because of the first decision. The approval of Obamacare was such a decision. More personally, a decision to get married leads a set of decisions very different from those to be made if the person were to stay single.

The most challenging of the path-dependent decisions are those that are not easily reversible. Once the decision is made and carried out, you are stuck with the consequences. A dramatic example of irreversible decisions was the decision by Hernán Cortés the conqueror of Mexico. In July 1519, he decided to sink his ships to prevent his men from changing their minds about attacking the Aztecs.[10]

2. Evaluate the Situation

The second step in making a decision is to evaluate the situation. Gather relevant information and use it to more fully understand the situation and the nature of the decision.

Include identification and testing of key assumptions in the evaluation. Include confirmation that the decision-triggering gap really exists and needs to be addressed now vs. delaying action.

3 and 4. Identify and Evaluate Possible Choices

The third and fourth steps of the decision process are to identify possible choices, then evaluate them. The manner of identifying and selecting can range from little conscious thought to careful deliberation. For minor, everyday, routine decisions, we are hardly aware the choice identification and selection is happening in our minds.

The choice identification and evaluation can be based on matching prior patterns. As noted earlier, the pattern-matching approach can work well if the decision-maker is sufficiently experienced and has a rich, varied set of prior experiences to use for evaluating choices. The pattern-matching approach can be disastrous when used by an inexperienced decision maker.

As noted earlier, Gary Klein has done extensive and interesting work on intuitive decision making, and his book, *Sources of Power*, provides useful insights on pattern-matching.[11]

With a more structured approach, you identify several choices and methodically evaluate them against measures of success. For example, consider the decision on how to invest your money. You first define your investment objectives. You then identify possible alternative portfolios of investments. Next, you evaluate the likely future performance of each portfolio in achieving your measures of success.

5. Select a Preferred Choice

The fifth step of the decision process is to select the preferred choice. If the selection is done properly, the choice will have a better chance of closing the perceived gap than any other choice of comparable risk.

Sometimes the best decision choice may be to do nothing. It can be prudent to put off decisions for a variety of reasons: no choices seem acceptable, the problem requiring a decision is unlikely to worsen soon, additional information is needed to make a good choice, the resources needed to implement the decision are not yet available, other decisions are more important, changing circumstances may close the gap for you.

The do-nothing choice, of course, must be chosen mindfully, not simply be the result of blindness or neglect.

6. Implement the Preferred Choice

Once a choice is made and course of action decided, the final step is to implement the choice selected. To implement business decisions well, lay out a schedule of implementation action steps, each with a target date and action-step owner, and set up a way to manage and communicate progress on the implementation.

In my experience, good implementation occurs less than half the time for both personal and business decisions.
Quite often, the implementation of business decisions is flawed because of poor planning, poor communication, poor organizational preparation, and weak leadership. These flaws are themselves the result of poor decisions,

another example of how bad decisions beget bad decisions.

Summary Thoughts on the Six Steps

The six-step process just described is how you make decisions when you use an analytical approach. Think about your recent decisions that involved some analysis. You will find that each of them follows the six steps.

You will probably find that you were more careful with decisions considered important than with more routine decisions. Would you also say that you did not spend much time thinking about the frames you used to set up the decisions? If so, you have a lot of company.

The Frame is the Key

To summarize the key message: a good frame is the key to decision success. It points you in the right direction.

If you had been the captain of the Titanic, a good frame would have focused your thinking on how to avoid icebergs, rather than on matters of less importance.

A good frame is shaped by using good assumptions, ones that are realistic, current, and relevant. Do the opposite of the captain of the Titanic who based his decisions on bad assumptions about the durability of the Titanic and the likelihood of encountering icebergs.

Good assumptions help you choose the right framing question, one that will focus the search for decision choices in fruitful directions. Good framing questions will also point to good success measures that provide correct criteria for evaluating the choices identified.

Frame choice has a much bigger impact on the quality of a decision than do the other five steps of the decision-making process. This is true not only because a good frame choice points you in the right direction but also because good frames strengthen every one of the six steps you use to make a decision.

Here's why. If you think about the steps in making a decision, each step itself involves decisions. Take the third step, identify possible choices. To carry out the step, one must make decisions: How shall you identify choices? Who should be involved in identifying the choices? When should you stop identifying choices and start evaluating? Or in short, what process should you use to identify choices?

Frame poorly these decisions about identifying choices, and you will end up doing a bad job of identifying. You are then likely to miss the best choices.

Frame Management -- The Five Skills

By now it should be clear: if you want better decisions, do a better job of finding and using good decision frames. As noted earlier, five skills enable you to use decision frames effectively:

1. Know Your Frame.

The first skill is frame awareness: Know the frame you are really using and be able to assess how good it is. What you need for this skill is covered in Chapter 2.

2. Manage Your Emotions.

The second skill is emotional awareness and control: Recognize your emotional state when you are making a decision, understand the effect of your emotions on the quality of your decision frame and on the quality of your decision. Control your emotions sufficiently to produce a good decision. The effect of emotions will surprise you. Chapter 3 provides the information you need on the emotional awareness and control needed for good decisions.

3. Shift Your Frame.

The third skill is frame shifting: How to shift your decision frame to a better one. This is the most important and most difficult of the five skills. Chapter 4 discusses how to shift the decision frame, why doing so is so difficult, and how to overcome those difficulties and find a better frame.

4. Manage Frames to Persuade and Negotiate.

The fourth skill is to use frames to persuade and negotiate more effectively. Decision frames are at the heart of all efforts to persuade and all efforts to negotiate an agreement. This skill is crucial to the success of any social interaction involving decisions and in particular, to efforts to implement change in your organization. Chapter 5 provides an overview of what is needed to manage decision frames for persuasion and negotiation.

5. Avoid Frame Traps.

The fifth skill is avoidance of frame traps. The traps are tricks your mind plays on you, causing you to think you have chosen a good frame when you have actually selected a bad one. Unless you are aware of them, these traps will bedevil you over and over again, leading to disappointing results without your understanding why they happened. In Chapter 6 you will learn the more common traps and how to avoid them.

Master the five skills and enjoy the better decisions that you make.

Better Business Growth

In too many businesses, mediocre decisions hamper the quest for better business growth. Equally, long-running patterns of superior growth have been broken by bad decisions. The batting average is not good. One of the most interesting things about Jim Collins' excellent book *Good to Great*[12] is not how eleven companies went from good to great. It is, rather, the fact that only 11 out 1,435 companies did it.

Dr. Collins offers interesting and provocative ideas for performance improvement, based on what he and his colleagues learned about the good-to-great companies. Unfortunately, none of his advice will work in the other companies Collins studied if the leaders of those companies use poorer quality decision frames.

Good decision frames are needed for two types of decisions related to business growth: (1) decisions about the process to use to search for growth ideas and (2) decisions about where to look for the best growth strategy.

The Journey to Better Decisions

In this chapter, you have learned the crucial role frames play in our lives. For good decisions, the choice of frame matters more than anything else. You have learned why this is so through a discussion of how we make decisions and the role of frames in the process. You also received several examples to illustrate the importance of frames.

The five frame-management skills will help you make better decisions. The remaining chapters will give you what you need to develop those skills.

We'll begin with the first skill—awareness of the frame.

2

KNOW YOUR FRAME

We think that what we see is what there really is.

John Sterman

Suppose you need to make an important decision. You want the decision to be a good one. What do you need to do first?

From Chapter 1, you know the answer. Check the decision frame you are using. The decision frame is essentially the way you describe the decision and its circumstances. Choose a bad frame, one that describes things incorrectly, and you will get a bad decision.

Making a decision with a bad frame is like trying to play golf with a baseball bat: the golf ball is unlikely to go where you want. Choose a good frame to make a good decision.

In this chapter and the next two, I will put the proper golf club in your hands. We will begin by taking a closer look at what a decision frame is. We will examine a decision frame's parts so you will know how to identify and assess them. In the next chapter, you will learn how emotions shape your choice of frame and your decision. In Chapter 4, you will learn how to change to a better decision frame and how to protect yourself from the very real barriers stopping you from shifting to a better frame.

To warm up your thinking on this, let's look at a case study--the bad frames used by Quaker Oats' management in the ill-fated acquisition of Snapple.[1] We will refer back to this case study as we explore how to choose good decision frames.

Snapple

In 1972, three New Yorkers believed that people wanted unadulterated fruit juices with all-natural ingredients, instead of the processed juices then commonly available. Thus, Snapple as a company was born, the vision of two brother-in-law window washers, Leonard Marsh and Hyman Golden, and a friend, Arnold Greenberg who owned a Manhattan health food store. They initially called their company Unadulterated Food Products.

The founders were not sure their venture would succeed, but it did. Their company rode the 1980's wave of increasing demand for natural products.

They first came up with the name Snapple for a carbonated apple drink. The name is a combination of the words "snappy" and "apple." Initial versions of the product were so snappy they blew off bottle caps if they got too warm. The founders liked the Snapple name, so they eventually made it their company name--Snapple Beverage Corporation.

Snapple Success

In 1987, Snapple started its line of ready-to-drink iced teas. Through the 1980's and early 1990's, Snapple's sales were growing briskly and the Snapple brand dominated the iced-tea drink market segment.

The Snapple brand had (and still has) a quirky, individualistic quality that appealed to a particular market. Snapple's advertising promoted that image, featuring "regular" people touting the drink. The most famous of these was a Snapple employee, Wendy Kaufman, a kind of Mrs. Every-Woman who appeared regularly in their company's television ads, responding to letters from fans.

The Snapple distribution system was as quirky as the brand, depending for success on a band of independent distributors who generated 80 percent of sales through lunch counters, delis, health food stores, and small groceries. Only 20 percent of its sales were. from the more common supermarket channel.

A Big Problem

As usual, success breeds imitators. Coca Cola, Pepsi, and several smaller companies introduced competing iced tea drinks. By 1994, Snapple had a big problem. It was losing market share, and the growth rate for the iced tea drinks category was beginning to slow from the very high rates (50-100% per year) of the prior five years.

At the same time, Quaker Oats also had a problem. Once just a cereal company, by 1993 it had become a large, diversified food manufacturer. Quaker's CEO, William D. Smithburg, had made his name by acquiring Gatorade in the early 1980's and growing the sports drink through effective marketing and distribution. By the early 1990's, Gatorade was the core of Quaker's performance, with consistent double-digit annual growth.

The problem Quaker Oats faced was the same as Snapple's, a slowdown in growth. This led Smithburg and his team to look for new acquisitions to sustain the growth. Snapple headed the list of acquisition candidates.

Win-Win?

Imagine you are in Mr. Smithburg's situation. You need to find a way to increase growth. Is a repeat of the Gatorade success possible? Can it happen with Snapple? , How would you have framed the decision on whether or not to acquire Snapple? What would your framing question(s) be? Let's examine what happened, then look at possible framing questions.

Failure

In 1994, Quaker Oats acquired Snapple for $1.7 billion. Smithburg and his team believed they could do for Snapple what they had done for Gatorade. Once they owned Snapple, the Quaker Oats team decided to pursue three initiatives that had worked well for Gatorade:

- Optimize distribution for both Snapple and Gatorade.

- Roll out large-size bottles of Snapple.

- Use non-controversial, more conventional ads.

These supposedly proven ideas turned out to be huge flops.

Snapple's distributors rebelled against the initiative to "optimize" distribution. Those distributors served lunch counters and delis. They were just beginning to penetrate supermarkets. Quaker Oats already had distribution to supermarkets and did not want the Snapple distributors to duplicate the existing system.

To placate the Snapple distributors, Quaker Oats, sensing synergy where none existed, offered them the opportunity to distribute Gatorade to their current outlets if they would stop trying to penetrate supermarkets. But the Snapple distributors knew they would make less money on each bottle of Gatorade sold than they would on each bottle of Snapple sold. They also knew Gatorade would not sell well in traditional Snapple outlets. The Snapple distributors saw no wins for themselves with Quaker Oats' distribution plan and blocked it.

The new large-size Snapple bottles didn't sell. Athletes want large Gatorade bottles. They need a lot of fluid to re-hydrate. Snack-oriented Snapple customers want smaller, more convenient sizes.

Quaker's conventional ad campaign did not work. Quaker dumped Wendy Kaufman and the effective, quirky Snapple ads for "safer" mainstream ads that were more bland and sophisticated, with no personality or warmth. The sterile, boring ads failed.

Four years after Quaker Oats paid $1.7 billion to acquire Snapple, the company sold Snapple to Triarc Beverages for just $300 million, a loss of $1.4 billion. And shortly after the sale, William Smithburg was no longer CEO of Quaker Oats.

Bad Assumptions - Bad Frame

Quaker Oats got in trouble because of a bad decision frame at the start of the acquisition process. I asked you earlier how the acquisition decision might have been framed. Here are some possible framing questions.

Should we acquire Snapple because...

1. it fits our strategy?
2. we can get it at a good price?
3. we can grow it the way we grew Gatorade?

Notice how each framing question emphasizes a certain aspect of the situation. The first focuses on fit with strategy, the second on price, the third on acquisition tactics.

The Quaker Oats' acquisition team, at one time or another, may have considered each of the questions, as well as others. But based on their post-acquisition behavior, I think it's likely that the third framing question dominated, and it shaped their thinking about the acquisition. The third framing question is a bad one. It prematurely assumes the acquisition is really a good idea and tends to imply what worked for Gatorade will work for Snapple. The third framing question diverts attention from challenging the merits of the acquisition and challenging the validity of the Gatorade-clone strategy.

In trying to grow Snapple, Smithburg and his team were aware of Snapple's peculiarities in terms of its quirky brand and its market outlets, but they seem to have been blind to the fundamental importance of these peculiarities. I believe pride plus the repeat-Gatorade frame trapped them into making the following assumptions:

- Our marketing methods will enable us to grow the brand.
- Our style of advertising will work better than Snapple's.
- We can create distribution synergies.

These were bad assumptions. The first two were based on Quaker Oats' experience in developing the Gatorade market. They downplayed the significant difference between the Gatorade and Snapple markets. The third was unrealistic because of differences between the Snapple outlets and distributors and those used for Gatorade.

Quaker Oats' bad framing question produced bad assumptions. The bad framing question, combined with bad assumptions, led to a bad decision frame and to bad decisions on the Snapple acquisition and how to grow

Snapple after the acquisition. The result was a financial disaster.

Because of the bad assumptions, Quaker Oats' executives thought they could grow Snapple the way they had grown Gatorade. Instead, from 1993 to 1997, Snapple's sales fell from $674 million to $440 million.

Triarc Does It Right

Quaker's executives ignored the crucial differences between Gatorade and Snapple because of their bad frame. With a better frame, Quaker Oats would have understood what those differences meant and could well have decided against the Snapple acquisition. If it had continued with the acquisition, a better decision frame would have led to a better strategy and a more successful outcome.

How do we know this? Because, as noted earlier, Triarc bought Snapple from Quaker Oats in 1997. Triarc's management chose a good frame based on the framing question: "How can we best leverage the intrinsic value of the Snapple brand?" The new frame led to strategic initiatives quite different from those Quaker Oats pursued:

- Try new flavors using low-cost tests, then run with those that look good.
- Bring back the warm, fuzzy ads.
- Use small-size bottles only.
- Win back the distributors alienated by Quaker Oats. Triarc restored Snapple's growth with these initiatives.

Three years after buying Snapple, Triarc sold the business to Cadbury Schweppes for $1.06 billion in 2000 for a 235% gain in just three years.

Triarc's frame was good, in part, because it was based on realistic assumptions about the nature of Snapple, its customers, and its distribution. And what a difference the better frame made!

Snapple is a useful example because it contrasts the effects of good and bad frames so well. Absent the contrast between Quaker's and Triarc's decisions, we might be tempted to say that Quaker executives made good decisions and just had a run of bad luck. But Triarc's excellent results indicate strongly that the highly talented Quaker executives really did make bad decisions, and those bad decisions were based on a bad strategic decision frame.

In the next section, I discuss how to identify and assess your decision frame so you will make decisions more like Triarc and less like Quaker Oats. I will use Snapple as an example throughout, but please recognize that this is my retrospective interpretation of what might have occurred. I have no direct knowledge of what actually occurred in the meeting rooms of either company.

Identify and Assess the Frame

The Snapple example illustrates the need for a good frame to make good decisions. You will make a better decision whenever you take care to describe the frame you are using and confirm that it is a good one.

As noted in Chapter 1, a decision frame has four features: the perceived gap, the framing question, the success measures for the decision, and the assumptions used. To describe the frame, describe each of the four features.

To assess the quality of the frame, assess the quality of each frame feature.

For most, this describing and assessing will be a new skill, one that greatly improves the way you formulate a decision. Because it is a new skill, you can expect to find it a little difficult and time-consuming at first. But after doing it just a few times, your skill will improve, and you will find that you can do it quite quickly.

Try the concepts I will describe shortly. Describe and assess simple decisions, such as how you to get to work each day, how you prioritize work for the day, where you go for dinner when you eat out, or what you and your family will do with your vacation time. This practice will improve your ability to tackle more complex decisions.

Much of the discussion that follows will be in terms of business activities. However, the ideas presented work for any type of organization, and for personal decisions related to you and your family.

Now, let's look at how to describe and assess the four features.

The Gap

The gap is a perceived difference between current conditions and what is desired. As noted in the first chapter, the existence of a gap triggers the impulse to make a decision. The purpose of the decision is to find a

way to close the gap. At Quaker Oats, the gap leading to
the Snapple decision was the perceived difference
between the company's slow rate of growth in the early
1990's and higher desired growth rate.   The Snapple
acquisition was seen as the way to help close the growth-
rate gap.

Without a perceived gap, we do not feel a need to
make a decision. Each day, every decision we make,
small or large, is triggered by a gap. Usually, we give little
thought to the gap. For major decisions, however, you pay
some attention to the gap.

Describe the Gap

To describe a gap, describe the current situation
and the desired situation the decision is to achieve. Then,
summarize the defects in the current situation the decision
must address.

Assess the Gap

Once the gap is defined, assess its validity,
importance, and urgency. To assess its validity, confirm
that the descriptions of the current and desired states are
accurate and complete. To what extent is the description
of the current state based on information of questionable

quality? Is the "desired" state really so preferable to the existing one? Is the desired state realistically achievable or will its pursuit create problems?

In the Snapple case, the information on the gap was valid. Quaker Oats had very good data on its growth. I believe that, for a number of sound business reasons, the company's management considered a higher level of growth to be of value and preferable to the current state. It is not clear whether the higher growth target was realistically achievable.

To assess the importance of the gap, evaluate the benefits of closing the gap. Compare those benefits with the consequences if the gap is not closed. If the benefits are a significant improvement, the gap is important.

In the Snapple case, to not close the growth-rates gap would hurt Quaker Oats' competitive position and stock price. Close the gap and the company's competitive position would strengthen and its stock price would increase. Clearly, the gap was important to Quaker Oats' leaders.

Assess the urgency of the gap-closing need. Explore the consequences of delay. It is easy to get caught up in the momentum of trying to close a gap once one is recognized.   It is better to first decide whether quick action is really needed.

It would not surprise me if the Quaker Oats executives were overly concerned about a quick fix to their growth challenge, and this fostered a sense of urgency about the Snapple deal.

If the gap is valid, important, and urgent, proceed with the decision-making task. Otherwise, wait. Clearly, Quaker Oats' executives might have benefited from waiting and considering other gap-closing options.

The Framing Question

The framing question is the most obvious and prominent feature of a decision frame. It is the question that characterizes the decision to be made. In the Snapple case study, I presented three possible framing questions Quaker Oats might have used, none of which is very good. I also described a good framing question, the one that Triarc probably used to succeed where Quaker Oats had failed.

Identify the Framing Question

To describe the framing question should be easy. Still, for group decisions, it may be useful to have everyone involved in the decision provide a separate version of the question and then compare them. Again, this reveals the extent of agreement about the framing question and may help lead to a better one.

Assess the Framing Question

A good framing question should satisfy four requirements:

1. Exposes a sufficiently wide range of options, rather than hiding them,
2. Does not prematurely assume the choice to be made.
3. Is based on a broader, systems-level perspective of the situation, rather than concentration just on the immediate circumstances,
4. In the case of a framing question about how to fix a problem, focuses on causes, not just symptoms.

Smithburg and his team at Quaker Oats appear to have been guilty of violating the second requirement. They would have used two related framing questions, one for the Snapple acquisition decision and one for the Snapple growth strategy. Their acquisition-framing question would have flunked requirement two because it presumed that the acquisition would be made, excluding the option of not doing the acquisition.

Their growth strategy question would have flunked requirement two because it presumed that the Snapple strategy would be similar to the Gatorade strategy. In giving prominence to a strategy that repeated what was done for Gatorade the team blinded itself to serious consideration of strategies that differed from the Gatorade approach.

In contrast, Triarc was not distracted by a history with Gatorade and chose a framing question for its strategy that allowed a wider range of choices and gave greater consideration to the unique growth opportunities in the Snapple brand.

Test your framing question against the four requirements. If it falls short on any of them, change it as needed until the four requirements are satisfied.

The Assumptions

Assumptions are the fourth feature of a decision frame. Three types of assumptions arise in making any decision:

1. gap existence confirmation,
2. framing question selection,

3. generated by the framing question.

Consider the gap-creating assumptions. If they are valid, they helpfully reveal that an important gap exists. If those assumptions are not valid, they create the perception of a gap and the need to act when no gap exists and no action is needed.

Think of the assumption that there is a fire near you when no fire exists. This is a false alarm that creates a false gap between your current state and desired state of safety. The fewer such false alarms the better. There was no false alarm in the Snapple case. The assumption that growth was too slow was valid, based on Quaker Oats' history, investors' expectations, and the performance of your firm's competitors.

Assumptions of the second type shape the framing question. If those assumptions are valid, the chances of choosing a good framing question are better. As discussed earlier, in the Snapple case, bad assumptions were used (Snapple is like Gatorade, Quaker Oats knows how to improve Snapple's performance, Snapple and Gatorade customers are similar enough, differences in the distribution channels can be managed, etc.). These bad assumptions led to a series of bad framing questions and bad decisions.

Assumptions of the third type are those that come to mind because of the framing question. These assumptions will affect the identification and evaluation of alternatives. Good framing questions lead to better assumptions than do bad framing questions. In the Snapple case, the bad framing question, "How can we succeed with Snapple like we did with Gatorade?" leads to assumptions such as the following: the Gatorade advertising approach should work, we can use Snapple distributors for Gatorade, and larger-size bottles of Snapple should be a hit.

Such assumptions were not valid and also narrowed the range of choices considered. I believe anything that was not a close variant of the Gatorade strategy was cut out. Thus, the best options never made it to the final list of potential strategies considered.

In summary, the assumptions used to formulate a decision will lead to a good or bad decision frame. Bad assumptions mean a bad decision frame, as the Snapple acquisition example indicates. Good ones may lead to a good decision frame, such as Triarc's.

The Assumptions Challenge

To formulate a decision properly, use good assumptions. Identify and assess the assumptions to be sure they are good ones. To identify assumptions can be difficult because many assumptions are hidden from conscious thought. They surround you, and you depend on them, like the air you breathe—without conscious awareness. Expose such hidden assumptions and your decision will improve.

Describe the Assumptions

To identify and describe the gap-creating assumptions, list the "facts" that convince you the gap exists. These "facts" will usually really be beliefs about what the current situation is and what the desired situation is. Not all of these beliefs will be valid. In the Quaker Oats case, the key and valid belief was a less than desired rate of sales and profit growth.

To identify assumptions that lead to the framing question, examine the way the decision is posed. Probe why it is posed that way. By so doing, you will uncover assumptions related to the nature of the decision. For example, the framing question "Where shall we go on vacation?" is created by the assumptions that you should have a vacation, that you should go somewhere on vacation, that you should not go alone, that the choice of where you go matters, and where to go is more important than other vacation considerations, such as what to do on vacation. Underlying these assumptions are assumptions about why going somewhere on vacation is so important and why different locations vary in attractiveness.

Now, let's consider the assumptions that get attention because of the framing question chosen. As noted earlier, the framing question leads to assumptions that influence the identification and evaluation of ways to close the perceived gap. There are many of these assumptions. The number may surprise you until you actually start identifying them for a decision you are making. Eleven categories of such assumptions are listed in Exhibit 2.1.

Use this list to help identify the important assumptions that you seem to be using. Pick the 8-10 assumptions that are most critical to the success, and assess these carefully. I discuss how to do the assessing in the next section.

Exhibit 2.1

Types of Assumptions Highlighted by a Framing Question

1. Boundaries on the search for choices (How far from business as usual?)
2. Time horizon for evaluation of choices (How soon must you pick?)
3. Individual or organization capabilities
4. What is fixed and what can be changed
5. The factors that keep things stable or cause changes to happen
6. The "rules of the game" (every organization or society has unspoken norms)
7. Likely behavior of others affected by a decision
8. Current and likely future conditions of the relevant environment
9. The nature and lag time of feedback effects a decision will produce
10. Key risks
11. Degree of knowledge about assumptions

Assess the Assumptions

Rate your assumptions against four criteria:

1. Up to date,

2. Realistic,

3. Necessary,

4. Supported by good evidence.

Be warned. It is easy to fool yourself in doing this assessment. You may create mental traps that prevent you from recognizing bad assumptions. I will go over some of these traps in Chapter 6 in detail, but here are some examples to give a taste of the traps.

First trap: our projections of future conditions are influenced too strongly by recent information. For example, if a company gets better earnings each quarter for three quarters it is easy to assume the next 2-3 quarters will produce further increases. This was the view of many in September 2008, just before the October 2008 economic plunge and subsequent financial panic.

Someone with a child who is well-behaved from the age of 10 to 12 can get trapped into thinking the good behavior will continue as the child becomes a teenager, sometimes a bad assumption.

Another common trap is to hold onto assumptions based on obsolete conditions. One who assumes there is a clear separation between work time and personal time is making such an assumption. What was valid in an era without smart phones, tablets, and other smart mobile devices is no longer true.

In checking each key assumption, look for obsolete information and look for information that contradicts each assumption. Challenge your degree of certainty about the assumption and information supporting it. Then, fix any assumptions that have flaws.

The Success Measures

There are two types of success measures for any major decision:

- success of the decision (outcome success),
- success of the process used.

Outcome Success Measures

Outcome success measures are implied by the perceived gap and the framing question. For the Snapple purchase example, outcome success measures might be a good return on investment, improved sales growth, and a higher common stock price. Additional success outcome measures for Smithburg might be to keep his job and to preserve his reputation.

Describe the outcome success measures for a decision you are considering. If a group is involved, each person should provide a separate list of measures. Then these should be compared to see the extent of agreement. Prioritize the final list.

The outcome success measures should meet four standards:

1. They are sufficient to describe success.

2. Each measure has a qualitative description and a measurable target.

3. Each measurable target can be tracked.

4. Each measurable target includes a deadline date.

Process Success Measures

The process success measures show how good the decision-making process is. A good process scores high on the eight features listed in Exhibit 2.2. Well-managed organizations use a debriefing session after major decisions to assess performance against the features. This is a good practice to imitate. The debriefing session should produce a plan to correct any process flaws.

Exhibit 2.2

Features of a Good Decision Process

1. Right people: The right people are involved in the right ways at the right time.
2. Right framing question: a good framing question is chosen.

3. Broad search for options: The search for decision choices is broad enough to uncover several different and equally attractive options.

4. Right pace: The search for choices is done without excessive delay.

5. Good evaluation: The evaluation of choices is thorough enough to confirm which one rates highest on the outcome success measures.

6. Good assumptions: The assumptions used have been sufficiently identified, described, and validated.

7. Good implementation plan: The plan for implementation of the decision choice has been properly developed and communicated.

8. Good implementation start: All steps necessary to start implementation have been done in a timely and effective manner.

Summary--Knowing Your Frame

The first skill of frame management is to describe and assess the decision frame you are using. With this skill, you can identify the frame for a decision and assess whether or not the frame is a good one.

As noted earlier, you will get better with this skill as you practice describing and assessing the frames of simple decisions you have made and are making. Try it.

Use Exhibit 2.3 below to guide your efforts:

Exhibit 2.3

Features of a Good Decision Frame

Perceived Gap
Valid, sufficiently important, sufficiently urgent

Framing Question
   Exposes a sufficiently wide range of options.
   Does not prematurely assume the choice to be made.
   Is based on a broader, systems-level perspective of the situation.
   Focuses on causes of problems, not just symptoms.

Assumptions
Up to date, realistic, necessary, supported by good evidence

Success Measures
They are sufficient to describe success.
Each measure has a qualitative description and a measurable target.
Each measurable target can be tracked from available data.
Each measurable target includes a deadline date.

Whenever your assessment reveals you have a bad frame, you will want to shift to a better frame. Emotions can sometimes make the shift difficult. In the next chapter I will describe these emotional roadblocks and provide suggestions for overcoming them. Then, in Chapter 4, we will explore how to improve your ability to shift to a good decision frame before making a decision.

3

EMOTIONS AND FRAMES

When a man is prey to his emotions,
he is not his own master.

Baruch Spinoza

No decision is completely rational. Your emotions at the time of a decision influence every decision you make. You view a difficult decision differently if you feel happy than if you feel depressed. The emotional state plays out first in how you frame the decision. In a state of panic, for example, the frame is usually, "How can I escape?" It is not, usually, "How can I improve the situation?"

Many people believe that they would make better decisions if they could avoid getting emotional. This is not true. As we will discuss shortly, without emotions, we have great difficulty making decisions. Without emotions, we cannot make complex decisions, and even if we could, the decisions would probably be bad.

Emotions should be recognized as an integral part of every major decision and managed properly to insure that a good decision is made.   Recognition and management of decision-related emotion is the second frame management skill. Master it and the quality of your decisions will improve.

Manage the emotions you feel when setting the frame of the decision, and also manage the emotions you feel when making the other sub-decisions that are part of the decision: the process to use, the identification of alternatives, the evaluation of alternatives, selection of the best option, setting the implementation plan. Emotions are present in each case. For good decisions, recognize and manage the emotions you are experiencing.

Now, let us look more closely at the relationship between emotions and decisions. We will identify what is needed to master this second frame-management skill.

The Goldilocks Effect

In one version of the Goldilocks fairy tale, Goldilocks sampled three bowls of porridge. One was too cold, one too hot, and one just right. That's the way it is with the emotions related to decisions. Too little emotion and our thinking is too "cold" to make a good decision, or any decision at all.

Too much emotion and our thinking is too "hot" to make a good decision. Just the right amount of emotion and conditions are just right to make a good decision. That is what I call the Goldilocks Effect and it is illustrated graphically in Exhibit 3.1.

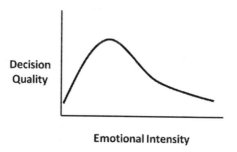

Exhibit 3.1—The Goldilocks Effect

Why do we have decision-making problems when there is no emotion? Psychologists have examined the decision making of people who lack the capacity to feel emotion due to brain damage. Two findings from this work relate to the Goldilocks Effect.[1]

First, people without emotions cannot make complex decisions at all! Faced, for example, with the decision of where to go to eat, they will endlessly ponder the pros and cons of one alternative after another without picking one. Scientists believe they do this because they have no way of prioritizing the pros and cons and no way of recognizing a superior choice. Why? Because we use emotion when we prioritize and when we select a preferred choice.

Second, in simple decision situations, requiring a choice of acting or not acting, people without emotions can make decisions, but the decisions are mediocre, and the decision-makers do not learn from their mistakes. These are the implications of experiments in which people without the capacity to feel emotions made repetitive decisions about two types of risky bets. One bet had good odds, the other poor odds. Normal people eventually recognize the poor bet and avoid it. People without emotion did not. They keep making the same proportion of bad bets even after many repetitions.

So, it is not a good idea to strive for a completely rational, Spock-like state when making decisions. The results will probably be bad.

It is equally true, and more obvious, that high emotion will lead to bad decisions. You have probably known someone who too quickly fell in love with another, resulting in a hasty act of commitment that led to bad results.

You have probably also known someone who too quickly fell in love with a particular stock investment, bought it, and waited for the stock's price to zoom up.

When, instead, the stock did nothing for a while and then started dropping, the hyped-up investor did what? Bought more! The stock kept falling. Then, the investor became stubborn and hung on. Finally, with the stock price down 90%, the investor bailed out. This was a typical pattern of decision making during the dot-com crash of 2000-2001 and the market collapse of 2007-9. This sad, and frequent, pattern of bad decisions is due to excessive emotions.

Excessive emotions clearly play a role when people are swindled. Even very intelligent, experienced, knowledgeable people can be taken when the scheme is sophisticated enough and their emotions blind them. A recent example is Bernie Madoff's long-running Ponzi scheme, which cost thousands of people a total, it is said, of around $50 billion.[2]

The folks who gave money to Bernie Madoff thought he would give them a modest, safe return through a clever investment strategy. They were blinded by emotions of smugness (feeling they were investing with the smart people) and affinity (we're tied with the good people because they are tied with Bernie). Compounding the effect of these emotions, was the presence of several mental traps that we shall go over in Chapter 6.

Too much emotion is bad for decisions; too little is bad. Your goal should be to seek and maintain the emotional level that leads to the best decision quality. I believe sane people, once they focus on their emotional level, can sense whether or not it is optimal for decision-making. However, if they are held too strongly in the thrall of an emotion, they will ignore their internal warnings and make a decision without reining in the emotions at play. As they say, act in haste, repent in leisure.

Make the effort to identify and regulate the emotions present during the making of a decision, both your emotions and the emotions of others involved. Your decision will be better.

And now for some bad news.

Limits on Emotional Control

Our efforts to attain and sustain an optimum level of emotion take work. It turns out our capacity to perform this work is limited. You can keep up the control for a time, but eventually, you use up your capacity, then you make dumb decisions.[3] If you stop trying to make decisions for a time, you replenish your capacity to control your emotions. It is as if your emotion controller is battery powered, and you must recharge its battery periodically.

This phenomenon explains the cause of many bad decisions. In an environment where difficult, stressful decisions are less frequent, our emotional control capacity fluctuates as shown in Exhibit 3.2a. The rest periods are sufficient to restore our control capacity.

However, when the tough decisions are frequent and the rest intervals small, our control capacity fluctuates as shown in Exhibit 3.2b. In this case, you do not have sufficient rest time to restore capacity and eventually use it up, after which decisions are made in an overly emotional state.

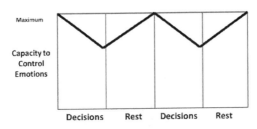

Time →

Exhibit 3.2a Adequate Rest Time to Restore Control

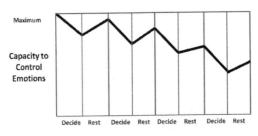

Time →

Exhibit 3.2b—Inadequate Rest Time to Restore Control Capacity

Examples come to mind: medical interns making bad diagnoses at the end of several 16-hour days in the emergency room, military commanders making poor decisions after several days of stressful combat, currency traders of large financial institutions losing hundreds of millions by making one decision too many, CEOs juggling too many balls for too long making dumb acquisitions.

In making a decision, assess your capacity to manage the emotions involved. If your capacity is low, either delay a decision or delegate it, if possible.

Decision Poisoners

Your choice of decision frame will be bad and your decision poor if your thinking is poisoned by emotion. The seven capital sins, in particular, will damage your decision-making. Pride (arrogance), lust, gluttony, greed, sloth, anger, envy-- reality is distorted and bad decisions follow when any one of these traits becomes strong in the mind of the decision maker. Add four more emotions – fear, depression, elation, and the yearning for comfort— and you have a checklist of 11 emotions to avoid.

Arrogance and greed blended with fear to shape the decision frames that led to the 2001 demise of the energy company Enron,[4] at the time, the largest bankruptcy in U.S. history.

Other energy companies, trapped by envy and sloth, pursued damaging imitations of Enron. In the early 1990's, the now-ironic term "Enron envy" was a commonly used expression in the industry.

Exaggerated pride plagues the acquisition efforts of many CEO's.[5]   The example of Newell Company is instructive.   Pride and lust were probably at work when Newell Company's CEO, John McDonough, decided in 1998 to acquire Rubbermaid.   The pride may have stemmed from Newell's long record of successful acquisitions, and the lust to do the deal[6].

Newell, a maker of house wares, had an excellent, 33-year record of uninterrupted growth achieved by its legendary leader, Daniel C. Ferguson. He grew the company by acquiring and "Newellizing" other companies, basically doing what many private equity firms do.   The long pattern of success, I suspect, led to an excess of pride in the company.

In 1997, John McDonough became CEO of Newell. I believe he may have lusted after Rubbermaid to show he could live up to the traditional standard set by Ferguson and Ferguson's effective immediate successor, William P. Sovey.

The decision frame McDonough used may have blinded him to the severity of the problems the acquisition would bring. Rubbermaid was far bigger than any previous acquisition, and Rubbermaid was in trouble because of its own poor decisions.

It appears that Rubbermaid management, because of *their* pride and obsolete assumptions, had never really accepted their loss of bargaining power to big-box retailers such as Walmart and Home Depot. In the 1970s and 1980s Rubbermaid was king. It had the bargaining power. Consumers coveted its brand. Retailers needed the products. But then competitive products gained ground and the big-box retailers started to dominate. It is likely Rubbermaid became mired in a bad, pride-blinded decision frame and made decisions that damaged its relations with companies like Walmart and Home Depot.

Newell was probably surprised by how badly the relations had been damaged and how severe Rubbermaid's internal problems were. Result: the "Newellizing" took four times longer and cost considerably more than expected.

The Rubbermaid acquisition derailed Newell's growth train, and today, nineteen years later, Newell still has not restored its historic growth pattern. In 1999, for the first time in 35 years revenues did not grow and excluding acquisitions, they have remained relatively flat since then.

Earnings fell from $1.94 per share in 1998 to $1.20 per share in 2001 and have remained flat since then. The stock price fell nearly 90 percent from early 1999 to 2008. And of course McDonough lost his job.

To avoid the eleven emotional poisons is simple, yet difficult. Just assess honestly if one or more of the emotions is shaping your decision frame. If so, work to moderate the errant emotions before making your decision. The difficulty rests in the words, "honestly" and "eliminate." The emotions themselves hinder an honest assessment and eradication of the problem. It can be very, very tough to do.

I have stressed the bad emotion-bad frame side of the situation. The pattern is the same for an excess of "good" emotions. For example, a decision frame shaped by overconfidence is also likely to be bad.

The Comfort Zone

Our ability to make good decisions is impeded to the extent that we want to stay in the comfort zone. If one views taking on a tough decision as unpleasant and discomforting, one may seek to avoid having to make the decision so as to remain in a state of comfort. This is an unhelpful kind of procrastination (there are helpful kinds, such as delaying a decision to cool down emotions or to gather valuable information).

A second dysfunctional response to unpleasant decisions is to rush them. Get the task done fast so you can return to the comfort zone. A hasty choice of frame, followed by a hasty selection of the "best" option, and hastily prepared implementation plan and you're done. Whew! And to repeat, act in haste, repent in leisure. These hasty decisions often turn out badly. It is just as well that the hastiness means their implementation will likely be botched.

It appears that hasty choices were abundant in the Obamacare website roll-out fiasco in the fall of 2013 and the subsequent bad decisions only made matters worse

A rush to judgment is particularly obvious in the identification of possible options for a major decision. After trotting out the most obvious choices, comfort seekers will shrink away from and curtail probing for more imaginative, but disturbing choices, thus missing out on the most transformative possibilities. It's just too unpleasant to think about them, particularly if the decision-making group is not schooled in *how* to think about them.

The pull of the comfort zone produces a third dysfunctional behavior: avoidance of disagreement. No one challenges the frame selected or the decision process to be followed. The decision-making group zooms in too quickly on one choice and goes with it. This behavior is one of the reasons people gave their money to Ponzi master Bernie Madoff.

Peter Drucker described an antidote to lack of disagreement. This was the method used by Alfred Sloan, Jr., the executive who, as noted in Chapter 1, led General Motors to greatness. Here is Dr. Drucker's description:

Alfred P. Sloan, Jr. is reported to have said at a meeting of one of the GM top committees, "Gentlemen, I take it we are all in complete agreement on the decision here." Everyone around the table nodded assent. "Then, "continued Mr. Sloan, "I propose we postpone further discussion of this matter until our next meeting to give ourselves time to develop disagreement and perhaps gain some understanding of what the decision is all about." [7]

Mr. Sloan's antidote is worth using to avoid the comfort trap. Don't settle for a decision choice until you have seriously considered, and then rejected, at least one other choice that is very different and equally attractive. Please note, this antidote is helpful, but it would not have stopped most of Bernie Madoff's victims from investing with him because those victims were also caught in the frame traps I will discuss in Chapter 6.

The Implementation Challenge

Guard against the debilitating impact of emotions on implementation of a decision, particularly when the implementation involves several people. Implementation involves sub-decisions: when to do implementation tasks vs. "regular" work, how to do the tasks, who should be involved, how to keep track of the implementation, and so on. If these sub-decisions are difficult to think about and challenging they can engender negative emotions—fear, frustration, feelings of inadequacy, a yearning for control.

These emotions can lead to all the problems discussed earlier: poor framing of the sub-decisions, procrastination, slapdash work, inadequate communication, insufficient monitoring of progress, and myopic thinking that focuses too much on the immediate and not enough on the long term consequences of actions.

At the start of an implementation effort, the emotion-linked problems usually are absent. But they emerge quickly once the reality of what is required sets in.

This is particularly true if the implementation plan and leadership are poor.

The more a decision choice to be implemented differs from business as usual, the more difficult the implementation will be, and the more likely it is that the effort will be poisoned by dysfunctional emotional reactions[8]. This is particularly true for major organization change initiatives and new strategies. To implement them, hard, focused thinking is needed for several years. And many in an organization see the implementation as a threat.

Control implementation problems due to dysfunctional emotions with the following actions.

1. Do a good job of implementation planning, including anticipating the kinds of emotional reactions the effort is likely to induce.
2. Create by your deeds and words a positive emotional climate for the change effort.
3. If an implementation team is involved, monitor closely how it is performing and take corrective action promptly.

Summary

You have seen in this chapter that emotions are an indispensable part of our decisions. To manage the emotions recognize them and regulate them so that they are as close to the optimum level as possible. Take advantage of The Goldilocks Effect. Since your capacity to control decision-related emotions can be used up, you must pace yourself. When you near the limits of your capacity, decisions should be deferred, if possible.

Be particularly watchful for the eleven emotions that poison decisions and make certain they are not shaping decision frames and decision process. And learn to avoid the temptation of the comfort zone when making decisions.

The implementation of a decision engenders its own set of sub-decisions. These can be made poorly if they are infected by dysfunctional emotions. Our vigilance with respect to management of the emotional climate, therefore, should be sustained until the implementation tasks have been completed successfully.

You have now learned (1) how to identify and assess the frame you are using for a decision, and (2) how to identify and manage the emotions that arise in setting a frame and making a decision. Now we are ready to learn the third skill: how to shift to a better frame.

4

FRAME SHIFT

We can complain because rose bushes have thorns, or rejoice because thorn bushes have roses.

Abraham Lincoln

Want to make a good decision? Start with a good decision frame. As discussed in Chapters 1 and 2, nothing else is more important for making a good decision. Know the decision frame you are using. Assess how good it is, using the approach described in Chapter 2. If the frame is poor, shift to a better one.

But be warned: The frame shift is not easy to do. Any frame shift is unsettling. Optical illusions illustrate what you are up against. Look at the picture in Exhibit 4.1 below.

Exhibit 4.1—Saxophone Player-Woman Illusion

Do you see a saxophone player or a woman? Whichever it is, continue looking until you see the other image. Notice the jolt you feel when you shift your frame from one image to the other. That is the jolt of a *small* frame shift, and it is not altogether pleasant. Major frame shifts, as you shall see, have a much greater impact on our minds.

There is a silver lining in this cloud, however. Notice that the more you flip the perceived images in your mind, the less severe the jolt. You can condition yourself to the phenomenon of shifting. As you do so, you can become more comfortable with the act, which makes it easier to identify and shift to better decision frames.

The optical illusion provides another insight. Notice how you make the shift from the saxophone player to the woman. For the saxophone player, you focus on the large black area.

For the woman, you focus on the white space to the right of the large black area. To make the shift, you give more emphasis to one thing and less emphasis to another. This is analogous to a shift from one decision frame to another: pay more attention to something not emphasized in the current frame and less attention to something currently on center stage.

Let's look at a second optical illusion to reinforce the points just made. In Exhibit 4.2, on the next page, do you see an old man, or a young couple kissing? Whichever you see, keep looking until you see the other image. Again, you feel a jolt with the shift. Again, to make the shift you focus more on certain features of the picture. What do you emphasize for the old man? What for the couple kissing?

Exhibit 4.2—Old Man-Young Couple Kissing Illusion

To see the old man, you focus on the bottom and the top of the image and pay less attention to the middle. To see the couple kissing, you focus on the center of the drawing and pay less attention to the top and bottom.

When you shift your perception in viewing the illusions you shift your frame. Frame shifting is a learned skill, the third, and most important, of the five skills needed to master the use of frames for better decisions. In this chapter, you will learn how to build this skill.

The Frame-Shift Challenge

Major shifts of decision frames are difficult. To shift from a poor decision frame to a better one, you must overcome three challenges:

The current mindset

Human psychology

Human physiology

The Current Mindset Challenge

If one has viewed reality the same way for a long time, a shift in perception and decision frame can be difficult.

The existing viewpoint and the decision frames it engenders are firmly entrenched in one's mind. Assumptions become dogma or, worse, invisible. The existing mindset shapes relationships in mutually reinforcing ways. The existing order carries a heavy legacy investment.

In organizations of all kinds (including families), a long-held, collective mindset becomes an accepted and compelling part of the culture. And again, assumptions become dogma, visible or invisible. Also, an individual's status and power in an organization are often perceived by the individual to be connected to the collective mindset. Members of an organization with high status and power, therefore, will be threatened by any shift away from the status quo and will resist it. I suspect such conditions have existed at General Motors for several decades and, as discussed in prior chapters, prevented GM's executives from making the decisions needed to avoid the 2009 bankruptcy.

Sydney Finkelstein explores characteristics of the obstructive corporate mindset in his book, *Why Smart Executives Fail.*[1] He notes that poor decisions and the inability to shift frames arise from four reasons:

1. Unrealistic mindsets,
2. Cultural bias of close-mindedness, which prevents questioning assumptions,
3. Communication failure between levels in a company,
4. Leadership egotism and hubris.

These four reasons reinforce each other. People in an organization do not challenge the unrealistic mindset because of close-mindedness. Ironically, people discount information that might lead to a new, better perspective precisely because it conflicts with the existing mindset.

People attempting to "rock the boat" with such information put themselves at considerable risk in companies with the four characteristics listed above.   Just look at what happened in August 2017 to James Demure at Google: ironically fired for publishing a memo contradicting the views of Google management about the presence of sexism. He had the audacity to suggest that differences between men and women could account for some discrepancies in job levels and pay.[2]

Poor communication between different levels of an organization worsens the failure to recognize a need to change.   For example, in a deficient business, sales people can get real-world signals that offerings are no longer valued, but little of this information gets to top management, and the little that gets through is dismissed due to pride and egotism.

A deficient organization mindset can make the organization particularly vulnerable to disruptive innovations since much innovation strikes at the heart of the existing order and calls out for radical frame shift.

Richard Foster notes that, "It is relatively easy to spot new technologies and decide to monitor or perhaps invest in them. What is much harder, indeed agonizing at times, is to stunt the growth of older technology by withholding development funds from it, even though progress can be made. People lose jobs, friendships are destroyed, often the entire business must change. These are facts you don't want to face."[3]

He is describing the barriers due to the existing mindset.

The movie *Moneyball* is an excellent true story, and an excellent example of how hard it is to shift a frame in your organization. It is 2002, Billy Bean is the manager of the Oakland A's baseball team, and he is in trouble. His player budget is only $35 million compared with the New York Yankee's $130 million. He just lost three good players and could not afford to buy new players of the same caliber. What to do?

Bean decided to shift to a new paradigm, one that would select and use players based on statistical analysis. With this approach he believed he could put together a team at low cost that equaled or exceeded the statistical performance of his previous team, even if the individual players selected seemed less talented.

All of his staff, except the statistician he brought on board, opposed the move. They fought with him over every player he suggested because, by their old beliefs, each was mediocre. And they fought with him over how the players would be used.

Bean prevailed. The new paradigm performed amazingly well, producing an unprecedented streak of 20 straight wins that propelled the lowly A's into the championship playoffs.

I highly recommend the film as a good tutorial on the challenges and benefits of good frame shifting.

Human Psychology Challenge

Psychological factors reinforce impediments to frame shifting created by the existing mindset. A number of mental traps make effective frame shifting difficult. A sample of these traps is presented in Chapter 6. Their net effect is to fool executives into thinking a bad frame is a good one.

Another psychological barrier is discomfort. A frame that challenges the existing order is uncomfortable, perhaps even perceived as threatening, as noted earlier.

Cross your arms the way you normally do. Now cross them the other way. It doesn't feel right, does it? That is how an unprepared mind reacts to the prospect of a frame shift: the effort is uncomfortable, and there is a strong tendency to retreat back to comfort. It takes an effort of will to overcome the comfort zone so one can shift to a better frame. See the discussion in Chapter 3 for more on the effect of discomfort on decision-making.

Human Physiology Challenge

The final impediment to shifting is physiological. Scientific evidence indicates that our brains have a property called neuroplasticity.[4] If you think in a certain way, certain areas of the brain are activated. Continue the way of thinking over a long period of time, and nerve cells in the active part of the brain grow more neurons and capillaries.

Findings from neuroplasticity research lead to the inference that you alter the structure of your brain through the repeated use of the same approach for making decisions.
You alter the structure in ways that make the habitual decision process easier to use. Any other decision-making

approaches will become more difficult to do than the habitual one and will require more effort.

Similarly, if one has a long-held mindset, the research findings imply the brain structure will change to facilitate the involvement of that mindset. A shift to a different mindset, on the other hand, will require more effort, and will, therefore, be uncomfortable and tiring.

People who practice a certain profession for many years, confront certain types of decisions in the same way over and over again. Over time, their brains become physically different from those of other people. The structure of a lawyer's brain will differ from that of a musician, for example.

Executives who use a certain decision frame repeatedly over many years alter their minds in favor of the frame.
The part of the brain focused on the frame receives a disproportionate amount of energy through the additional capillaries.

These same executives, when required to think about and try a new frame, are being asked to activate a previously less-used part of the brain, one relatively deficient in neurons and capillaries per nerve cell. The result is that thinking with a new frame is tiring. Not enough energy flows to the nerve cells being used for the new thinking.

This brief discussion of the three types of frame-shift challenges indicates that frame-shift thinking is tiring and uncomfortable, and organizational resistance to a frame shift is high. It should be no surprise that the success rate of successful frame shifting is low. It's like asking a golfer who has never played tennis to do so. Don't expect automatic great performance or enthusiasm.

Organization Life-Cycle Effect

There seems to be a relationship between an organization's position in its life cycle and the ability of its management to shift decision frames about strategy.

At the start, when the organization is a gleam in someone's eyes, the capability to shift is widely divergent. Some entrepreneurs hold fast to their initial concept and the decision frames it engenders. Others, like Walmart founder Sam Walton, do a lot of shifting.

As an ultimately successful organization takes root and begins to grow, it appears that the frame shift capability, at first, increases, and much experimentation takes place.

Over time, however, after a long period of success based on a particular business concept and its associated decision frames, the capability to shift frame often declines. Belief in the current organization concept and the decision frames associated with it becomes entrenched dogma. Also, the minds of the organization's leaders may be altered over time by repeated use of the frame, making shifting more difficult.

For awhile, the repeated adherence to a particular, successful concept will cause no harm, and in fact, is probably beneficial to performance in many ways. This benefit comes at a cost. Frame shift capability is reduced. This means the organization will be less able to cope when the easy growth ends, and the organization's performance begins to stagnate.

Throughout an organization's period of stagnation and then decline the internal frame-shift capability tends to remain weak. The organization's ability to adjust is hampered by its lack of frame-shifting skill. General

Motors, Eastman Kodak, the Veteran's Administration, and Research In Motion (Blackberry) are vivid examples of these points. Ultimately, such organizations may cease to exist and be supplanted by something more effective, having served their social purpose. That is the virtue of capitalism, painful as it might be to the people in the organizations that disappear.

Of course, there are many exceptions to this pattern, and I will give examples of them in the next section. But the pattern is common enough to provide a warning: leaders of any organization should work actively to achieve and maintain a high-level capability to shift frame if they want to prolong the health of their organization.

Successful Frame Shifts

We will look at four examples to show that successful frame shifts can be done: Howard Johnson Sr., Darwin Smith at paper-maker Kimberley-Clark, Gordon Moore and Andy Grove at Intel, John Chambers at Cisco.

Howard Johnson[5]

Howard Johnson Sr.'s success in growing his business in the period from 1925 through 1960 is due to several successful frame shifts. When confronted with the poor performance of his initial drugstore venture, I believe he shifted his frame from "How can I improve the performance of the store?" to something like "What would make the store special and unique?" The new frame led him to the idea of offering great ice cream in 28 flavors, unheard of in the 1920's. When the ice cream succeeded, he did not continue with a frame like "How can I increase sales in the drugstore?" He shifted to "How can I make more ice cream sales?" He eliminated the self-imposed constraint of focusing only on the drugstore and opened several ice cream outlets, all of which succeeded. Then, with a third frame shift, he opened his first restaurant, and the Howard Johnson's chain was born.

Darwin Smith and Kimberly-Clark

In *Good to Great*, Jim Collins identifies 11 companies that succeeded in moving from good to great performance[6]. These companies succeeded because their CEOs were great frame shifters. Collins describes how Darwin E. Smith stoked growth at Kimberly-Clark after he became CEO of the paper company in 1971.[7] At the time

Kimberly-Clark was a typical integrated paper company, covering every step from tree to sheet of paper and with a presence in most paper markets.

The strategic decision frame in the company, prior to Smith's leadership, was probably something like "How can we perform better as the integrated paper company we are?" From Collins' description of how Smith transformed your company, I infer he shifted to a different decision frame, something like "Where must we focus to create the most value?"

The old frame assumed the existing business structure and market coverage were "givens" that were just taken as the way things were and perhaps, if thought about, considered untouchable. Smith exposed and challenged the "givens." He, in effect, said nothing is sacred and chose a decision frame reflecting this assumption.

This frame led him and his team to exit key parts of the original and core business, moving out of the coated paper market and selling off the company's paper mills. They focused entirely on the consumer paper-products market, increasing investment in brands like Kleenex and Huggies.

Smith's shift was bold. It contradicted conventional "wisdom" and was widely criticized, but the decision was excellent and paid off dramatically.

During Darwin Smith's tenure as CEO, from 1971 to 1991, Kimberly-Clark' grew revenues and profits much faster than its competitors. Its common stock price rose twenty-fold, from $2 to $40 a share, a growth rate of 15% per year.

Review the other good-to-great examples in Collins' book. In each case, see if you can identify the old frame used for strategic decisions and the new frame the CEO induced by a frame shift. Then, describe, how the frame shift was done. What part of the old frame was changed to create a new frame? This "homework" is well worth doing to understand how to shift a frame. In the Kimberly-Clark case, the change in frame was an expansion of the scope of what could be challenged.

Gordon Moore and Andy Grove at Intel[8]

In the early 1980's, Intel's leaders viewed their company as a maker of memory chips and microprocessors. In the early 1970's, memory chips had driven the company's prior growth. Later, the microprocessor business became more prominent. The old frame guiding top-management decisions was something like "How can we maximize the performance of both product lines?" But this old frame was not leading to decisions that cured Intel's major problems.

Moore's Law (which Gordon Moore had famously pronounced twenty years before) describes the forces threatening Intel. The capability (speed and storage capacity per unit volume) of all things electronic was doubling about every 18 months, while manufacturing costs were being cut in half at the same rate. These forces were rapidly turning the memory chips into a commodity business, eroding margins rapidly. The Japanese were taking market share steadily, with lower-cost, better-quality memory chips.

In response to this threat, Moore and Grove shifted their frame. In 1985 Andrew Grove asked "If we got kicked out and the Board brought in a new CEO, what do you think he would do?" Gordon Moore's response was "He would get out of memories." Grove then said "Why shouldn't you and I walk out the door, come back in, and do it ourselves?"

For them, nothing was sacred, just as with Darwin Smith at Kimberly-Clark. Using their new frame, Grove and Moore exited the memory business and focused on microprocessors.

The frame shift was not easy to do. Moore and Grove had to deal with the kind of resistance Billy Bean faced when he shifted the frame at the Oakland A's. But they prevailed.

The result? The Intel frame shift unleashed extraordinary growth. From 1983 to 2000, annual revenues rose from $1 billion to $30 billion, profits from $100 million to $8 billion, and the stock price rose 50-fold, from $2 per share to $100 per share.

John Chambers at Cisco[9]

Throughout the 1990's John Chambers, the CEO of Cisco Systems Inc. made decisions using the frame "What technology do we need to continue our growth and where do we get it?" Cisco makes leading-edge Internet networking products, and throughout the 1990's experienced enormous growth, 40-50% per year, fueled by 200 acquisitions made in response to the "...where do we get it?" decision frame.

Cisco's growth slammed to a stop in 2001 when the dot-com bubble burst. Cisco's operating margin fell from over 20% to just 10%.

Chambers realized his strategic decision frame needed to be changed. Cisco's survival was at stake. He shifted to a decision frame something like "What must we do now to optimize Cisco's performance and maintain its technology leadership?"

This was probably a very difficult frame shift for Chambers, given Cisco's prior performance trend and Chambers' revenue-growth-oriented leadership style. But he succeeded.

The frame shift led to more emphasis on Cisco's internal processes, which were not very efficient. The lack of efficiency was a tolerable condition in days of fat margins and great growth, but not when margins and growth shrank.

The new focus led to a fiscal "diet and fitness" program that improved operating margins from the 10% of 2001 to over 30% in just two years. And growth resumed, but at a more modest 10-15% per year rate.

Shift Your Frame

How do you shift to a better frame?[10] The examples just cited demonstrate two approaches:

(1) change the framing question, and/or

(2) identify and challenge one or more key assumptions.

Howard Johnson changed the frame question by shifting focus from performance to what would make the store unique and valued. He made his second shift by challenging the assumption that the existing store should be his focus, shifting to, I imagine, the framing question "How can I maximize the potential of my great ice cream beyond just this drugstore?" This led him to the idea of setting up several ice cream outlets.

At Kimberly-Clark, Darwin Smith shifted frame by not accepting anything as given. He sold off the "crown jewels" of your company and freed it to grow at an extraordinary pace.

Review the other two examples. How did the business leaders change their strategic decision frames? You will find they altered the framing question and/or changed key assumptions.

How should *you* shift to a better decision frame? For quick, simple decisions, just do a quick check of the current frame as described in Chapter 2. Very often, just making yourself aware of the current frame can lead you to a better one.

For tough and important decisions, time spent finding the right frame is well invested. To shift your frame for a tough decision, imitate the practices just described in the examples above. Explore changes in the framing question and identify and challenge key assumptions. You will find that changing the question reveals assumptions to be challenged, and challenging assumptions reveals new framing questions.

To shift the frame for a tough decision, don't just shift to the first new frame you identify. Instead, identify several new frames, then pick the best one.

Throughout the process of seeking a new decision frame for a tough decision, keep in mind what I discussed in Chapter 2: maintain the right level of emotional involvement as you search for a new frame. And shift your frame about the search process if necessary. View it as a positive, opportunistic activity, not an unpleasant chore.

Now let's dig into a little more detail on how to shift the frame for tough decisions.

Change the Question

You can change the frame by changing the framing question. Here, for reference, is a list of ways to change the question:

1. Change the key adverb. For example, in the framing question, "Where shall we go on our vacation?" the key adverb is the word "where." Change it to how or when and you have different framing questions: How shall we go on our vacation? When shall we go on our vacation? Or take a business example. Shift from "Where shall we expand for growth?" to "How shall we expand for growth?" or "When shall we expand for growth?"

2. Change the key verb and adverb. Instead of "Where shall we go on our vacation?" try "What shall we do on our vacation?" The verb "do" replaces "go," and the adverb "what" replaces "where." For the business example, shift from "Where shall we expand for growth?" to "What do we need to do to expand for growth?" The verb "do" replaces "should" and the adverb "what" replaces "where."

3. Eliminate the adverb. Instead of "Where should we go on vacation?" use "Should we go on vacation?" Instead of "Where should we expand for growth?" use "Should we expand for growth?"

4. Change the object. For example, replace the object "vacation" with "paid time off" as in "Where shall we go on our paid time off?" Notice how this change frees you from assumptions about time use that are implied by the word "vacation." For the business example, replace "for growth" with "to best serve our customers" as in "Where shall we expand to best serve our customers?"

5. Expand the scope of the question. Instead of "What shall we do on our vacation?" try "What shall we do with the vacation we have each year for the next five years?" Or "What is the best way we can use the vacation time for each member of our family?" For the business example, instead of "Where shall we expand for growth?" use "What is the best sequence of markets to expand into for growth?"

6. Incorporate a higher-level objective in the question.
For example, "How can we use the vacation time to improve our cooking skill?" Or, "Should we use our vacation time to improve our cooking skill?" For the business example, "Where shall we expand for growth that best supports our mission?"

As you identify possible questions, some will sound more important than others. Some will sound like they should be answered before others. It can sometimes be valuable to arrange the set of questions identified in terms of sequence and priority. In some cases, you will end up expanding the original single framing question into several related questions, which may be the best way to proceed.

Identify and Challenge Assumptions

Assumptions are associated with any framing question. "Where shall we go on vacation?" implies the following assumptions:

- We should go somewhere on vacation.
- We will have a vacation.
- We will go on vacation together.
- We *can* go somewhere on vacation.

Challenge each assumption and you will uncover another framing question.

Take the first assumption. The challenge is "Why should we go somewhere for vacation?" This is really another framing question, one that leads to consideration of the pros and cons of a trip versus other uses of the time. Your assessment might lead to a different use of the vacation time.

For the business example, the framing question, "Where shall we expand for growth?" implies at least the following assumptions:

- We can expand for growth.

- We should expand for growth.

- We should do the expansion now.

- If we expand, we will grow profitably.

Related to these assumptions will be others about performance of your firm's products and services, capability to manage expansion, financial resources, ability to handle competitive responses, and so on.

Examination of these assumptions may show some are bad and may lead to assumption changes that shift the frame.

Choose the Best Frame

For tough decisions, identifying different framing questions and challenging assumptions will build greater knowledge of the decision and its context. This knowledge provides a good foundation for choosing the best decision frame.

To choose the frame, first summarize which assumptions are valid. The assumption challenge will have revealed that some original assumptions were incorrect. These are replaced with correct assumptions.

Now, organize the possible framing questions. Which questions are good ones to start with? Which should be answered after the starting questions are answered?

Choose from the starting questions the one that you believe has the best chance of closing the gap that engendered the need for a decision in the first place.

At this point, if you have done the question and assumption work properly, your informed intuition can do a good job of selecting the best framing question. If you have not done this work, your intuition will not have sufficient information to make a good choice.

Once you have chosen the best framing question, proceed with the other decision steps: identify and evaluate alternatives, choose the best, reconfirm that now is the time to act, and set a plan to implement the best choice.

Summary

To shift a decision frame is not easy. It is an uncomfortable experience at first. The effort is impeded by the existing mindset, by psychological effects, and by our physiology. Business examples of successful frame shifts show that changing the framing question and/or challenging key assumptions achieve the shifts. This is the process you should use to shift your decision frame.

The examples also reveal a quality in the people who make successful frame shifts—courage. You will need courage to shift the frame of an important decision. But the results will be worth it.

As noted earlier, shifting decision frames is a learned skill. Most people are not good at it until they have practiced shifting frames a few times. Build your skill with the process by using it on "safe" decisions. As you become more familiar with the process, you will find it becomes faster and easier to use. You will then be able to very rapidly identify new framing questions, identify and challenge key assumptions, and find a better framing question, the key to better decisions.

5

PERSUADE AND NEGOTIATE

But politics is not about facts. It is about what politicians can get people to believe.

Thomas Sowell

Without the ability to persuade one another, we would still be huddled around fires in caves. We might not even have fire. Without persuasion, there can be no change and no progress.

Most people are conservative. They tend to prefer the status quo, however miserable it may be. They must be persuaded, or forced by cataclysmic events, before they will exert the effort, change from the status quo, change behavior, direction, beliefs, or practices. Anyone who has implemented successfully a major change in a family, corporation, or other organization understands this need for persuasion.

The word "persuasion" can have negative connotations, and with some justification. Many times, attempts to persuade are done for reasons not in the best interests of the person being persuaded. But persuasion is also often a well-intended and good act, and as just noted, is necessary for progress.

You cannot persuade people without shifting their perceptual frames. Frame shift is the means by which persuasion occurs. If people think everything is okay when it is not, they must be convinced that things are not okay. Their perception must be shifted until they believe they are confronting a serious gap between what they have and what they want. If they are pursuing a fruitless course of action, they must be persuaded to shift to a new course of action that will be more likely to close the gap.

Of course, the comments in the previous paragraph assume the persuader is correct about the gap and the course of action. If the persuading person has followed the advice in the prior chapters, the odds of being correct are better for the persuader than for the people to be persuaded. On the other hand, if the person is wrong and a good persuader, trouble will follow. You can supply your own examples to confirm this point.

Negotiation is a special case of persuasion in which all parties to the negotiation attempt to persuade one another. Negotiation is an ever-evolving dance of frame-shift gambits.

The frame shifting needed to persuade and negotiate is the fourth frame management skill. This skill includes

(1) the ability to use frame shifts to persuade others and carry out successful negotiations, and

(2) the capability to detect and respond appropriately to persuasion-related frame shift efforts of others.

In this chapter, I describe the use of frame shifts for persuasion and negotiation and provide recommendations to build this skill. I do not presume to think this material is anything but a discussion of one small, but important, aspect of persuasion and negotiation. There is a large body of research and literature on both subjects with many useful ideas.[1] What I have not seen is any explicit descriptions of the crucial role frame shifts play, although that role is implied in many of areas of the research, such as game theory, for example. This chapter adds an explicit description of the role of frame shifts to the literature on persuasion and negotiation.

Shift Frames to Persuade

Gordon M. Bethune faced a persuasion challenge in 1994 when he became CEO of Continental Airlines. Continental had just emerged from bankruptcy for the second time, and it was on the brink of going back into bankruptcy yet again, this time fatally.

While the company was sinking, its managers and workforce were focused on internal political fights, not performance. Turf issues and cost cutting got top priority.

Here is how Bethune viewed the situation:[2]

Let me tell you the story of the ambulance in the valley. There's a little town, and it's about halfway up a mountain on a bend in the road. That hairpin turn is a terrible hazard, and about once a month, cars go flying off into the valley below. It's awful.

The town council gets together and they look into how much it's going to cost to regrade the road, put in signs, and install a guardrail--in other words, make the thing safe. Well, it's going to be really expensive. In fact, it's going to be so expensive that they decide they just can't afford it. But the cars are still flying off the road, and people are getting hurt. They don't like that, and they want to do something, so they solve the problem of the dangerous road in what they believed was a less expensive way.

They put an ambulance in the valley.

It's a great story, because it shows how hard people will work to avoid solving their real problem. At Continental before I came here, that kind of thinking was a way of life. The philosophy was that you couldn't solve a problem because it was too expensive to do what would solve the problem.

That's sort of where Continental was: It had become a lousy, unreliable airline, and people had stopped using us and for good reason. An airline has no real value at all unless it's predictable and reliable, but for a decade management had been cutting costs so much that it not only wasn't improving the road, it had even stopped putting the ambulance in the valley.

Bethune had to shift the company's focus from myopic cost cutting to performance improvement. The old Continental was stuck in a plunging death spiral of cost cuts leading to poorer flight reliability and service, leading to more customer defections, leading to lower revenues, leading, of course, to more cost cuts.

Bethune recognized that Continental needed to shift its focus away from costs to exit from the spiral. His goal was to shift the focus to how to improve its reliability and service and how to increase sales by revising its route structure.

To persuade Continental's people to make the frame shift he (1) made the survival threat visible and disturbing, (2) sold the benefits of working together to improve reliability and customer service, and (3) eliminated managers who could not make the mental shift.

His efforts paid off. In one year, Continental's income went from a loss of $6.31 per share to a profit of $2.54 per share, and common stock price from $3 to $22.

Continental sustained healthy profitability and grew revenues at seven percent per year for the next six years. None of this would have been possible without the frame shift due to Bethune's persuasion. The new frame also helped Continental weather the disastrous impact on air travel of the September 11, 2001 World Trade Center attack, an event which for a time cut the legs out from under the U.S. airline industry.

The Continental example illustrates the actions needed to persuade a group to change their frame. Four steps are required.

1. Understand the current decision frame and the assumptions related to it.
2. Define a new, better decision frame.
3. Identify assumption changes implied by the new frame.
4. Design and conduct a campaign to shift the group's decision frame.

Let's look at these steps more closely:

1. Understand the current decision frame

To do the first step, understand the current situation, describe the current perceived gap and decision frame using the methods described in Chapter 2. In Continental's case before Bethune, the gap was seen as one of costs being too high, which led to the framing question "How can we reduce costs?' This frame neglected customers and good marketing. Success was measured by short-term cost reductions. Two key assumptions were (1) efforts to improve services will cost too much, (2) the current route structure cannot be changed. These assumptions pointed to cost cutting as the only sensible way to save your company.

2. Define a new, better decision frame.

To do the second step, first find the more general gap that created the perceived gap. Identify the general gap by asking questions about the perceived gap. Why did costs need to be lowered? Because costs were too high relative to revenues. Why were costs too high relative to revenues?
Because Continental was not performing well enough to attract sufficient business to be profitable. The more general gap, then, was a performance gap, the gap between the performance needed for profitability and the current poor level of performance.

From the more general gap derive a new narrower gap, one that focuses in a better direction, a direction with a better chance of success. In the Continental situation, the new gap and the framing question become almost synonymous. Bethune changed Continental's gap from one of costs being too high to one of operating performance being too poor. This gap shifted focus from high costs to poor business processes.

To complete the frame shift, identify a new framing question based on the new gap. At Continental, Bethune wanted to persuade the workforce to shift to a frame based on the new framing question "How can we improve performance in ways that increase revenues and profits?"

3. Identify changes in assumptions.

To do the third step, first list the key assumptions on which the new decision frame is based. For Bethune's frame these were:

1) no survival without better operating performance,
2) success comes from working together for the customer,
3) we <u>can</u> change routes to focus on the best markets.

Then, compare the current frame with the new frame. Identify the most-critical flawed assumptions of the current frame. Lay out a plan to change the flawed assumptions. There are four potent mechanisms for doing so:

1. Expose the deeper beliefs underlying the current assumptions and prove that those beliefs are wrong.

Continental's history of 10 years of failure trying to cut costs was sufficient proof that cost-cutting was the wrong focus. Bethune also showed that process improvements could increase operating performance without increasing costs.

2. Demonstrate that what is believed immutable can be changed. Bethune led the change in route structure that eliminated low-performing flights and locations while increasing availability in high-demand markets. Revenues rose dramatically.

3. Raise the visibility and importance of assumptions that have been overlooked or given lower-priority. Bethune raised the visibility and importance of the assumption that working together for the customer was necessary for survival, an assumption that had been ignored for 10 years.

4. Change the yardstick used to measure success. Bethune emphasized performance yardsticks: on-time arrivals and departures, fast turnarounds at airports, high flight occupancy. The new yardsticks changed the focus of the people in Continental.

4. Design and conduct a change campaign.

Include in the campaign the following key activities:

1. Communicate early, often, and vividly the new gap and decision frame.

2. Expose false old assumptions and demonstrate repeatedly why they are wrong.

3. Identify and recruit to the cause a sufficient number of managers who believe and support the new focus.

4. Bring the people of your organization together to identify and implement ways to close the newly perceived gap.

In designing and carrying out the frame shift activities, understand the viewpoint of the people to be persuaded.

See through their eyes what the situation looks like. Use their perspective to test the effectiveness of different approaches for shifting the frame.

Once the change campaign is planned and launched, stay on course. Usually, a sustained effort of 2-3 years is required for major frame shifts.

Executives who seek to implement change are always faced with a challenge like Gordon Bethune's. The greater the deviation of the change from the current pattern of behavior, the greater the challenge will be. The preparation steps and campaign suggestions will help meet that challenge.

Shift Frames to Negotiate

Let's begin with an example of how not to negotiate:
the 2003 labor negotiations between Southern California grocery chains and the United Food and Commercial Workers Union[3]. The two parties failed to reach agreement on the Union's contract. The Union and related parties, 70,000 in total, went on strike. The strike lasted almost five months. It cost the grocery chains about $300 million in lost profits and even more in lost future revenues due to customer defections. It cost the workers five months of severely reduced wages and considerable stress.

In the settlement agreement to end the strike, the Union gained nothing. It basically agreed with the supermarket chains' original proposal, a proposal which had caused the strike in the first place. The strike was the result of poor negotiation skill by both parties, and it hurt both parties. There were no winners, just losers.

What went wrong? It appears that the grocery executives failed to understand sufficiently the decision frame of the Union's membership. Workers at the chains received good wages for modest skill-level jobs. Checkout staff, for example, could earn as much as $16 an hour ($23 per hour in 2018 dollars).

Even more generous, the chains paid all health insurance costs for workers and their families. And health care costs were growing 7-10% per year. The workers were receiving pay increases each year that far exceeded inflation when the health benefits were included.

Unfortunately, the workers, like most workers, thought of their pay in terms of the amount on the check they received, not their total compensation. The health benefits were not seen as compensation in their decision frame.

The workers wanted to at least keep the status quo. In contract negotiations, the chains proposed that workers pay $5 per week toward their health care. It appears that the workers viewed the proposal as a cut in pay. It was really an <u>increase</u> in pay (albeit, at a slower rate)! The workers were blind to what their total compensation was when health benefits were included.

From my experience with executives, I think the grocery-chain executives failed to understand sufficiently the decision frame the workers were using. If they had understood and had conducted a strong campaign to shift the workers' frame, the odds are good they would have averted the costly strike.

Of course, the Union's leadership had *their* decision frame regarding the proposal. Their frame would have been based on assumptions about what the Union leadership needed to do to keep its power, look good to the membership, and present a strong front to the grocery executives. It seems their frame was also based on distrust of the executives' intentions.

I suspect the grocery executives understood the frame of the Union leadership better than they did that of the workers, but they may have been using a poor frame in responding to the Union leadership. I lack sufficient information to assess whether a frame shift regarding how to interact with the Union leadership would have helped the negotiations, but I suspect it would have helped. And shifting the workers' frames would certainly have helped.

The supermarket strike illustrates one of the many ways negotiations can fail when the parties do not pay attention to the decision frames involved.

Negotiation involves two or more parties trying to persuade one another. Each party has its own frame, built around a framing question, "How can I persuade the other parties to agree to X?"

Each party has its own success measures and assumptions. The assumptions relate to the following:

1. The decision frame being used by each party.
2. The emotional state of each party.
3. What each party wants (success measures).
4. How each party views the other parties.
5. The actual and perceived relative bargaining power of each party.
6. The deadline perceived by each party for completing negotiations.
7. The extent to which each party will lower its demands.
8. How much each party values the object of the negotiation.

When one party's frame is shaped by bad assumptions, as was the case in the grocery chain example, the outcome of the negotiation is likely to be poor for that party and possibly all parties to the negotiation.

As these observations indicate, to prepare for successful negotiation you should answer the following questions:

1. What frame are you using? Should it be changed?

2. What are the frames of other parties to the negotiation?

3. What is the emotional state of other parties to the negotiations?

4. Can frame differences impede successful negotiations?

5. What frame shifts might move all parties forward toward an agreement?

For significant negotiations, good preparation is absolutely essential. Preparation includes the activities just cited, as well as role-playing, with some team members taking the part of the other parties to the negotiation. Preparation also includes deciding on the best alternative to not agreeing with the other party.[4] Identification of this alternative will help to establish a better decision frame and emotional state for the negotiation.

During the negotiations, be alert for efforts by the other parties to shift your decision frame. They will do this by emphasizing certain assumptions or success measures and downplaying others. Here's a simple example: about twenty years ago a securities broker was trying to persuade me to switch to electronic monthly statements, rather than have them mailed to me. He emphasized the assumption that I was at risk to identity theft with the mailed version. He was careful not to mention the extensive and increasing amount of online and wireless identity theft that was occurring, but I was aware, so his persuasion effort failed. I did eventually switch to digital statements, but more for convenience than differences in security.

Once you identify the manner in which other parties are seeking to shift your frame, ask yourself what assumptions they are downplaying. Assess the validity and importance of these downplayed assumptions.

Then decide whether or not to adjust your frame in the direction the other party seeks.

In some cases, it may make sense to do so because the adjustment will lead to a better frame (as defined in Chapter 2) and help the negotiations. In other cases, you will recognize that the shift the other parties seek will not lead you to a better decision. In such cases, you will therefore keep your original frame for judging offers and counteroffers in the negotiation.

Your goal throughout should be to use good frames for deciding on offers and deciding how to conduct the negotiations. The frequency of success will go up when good frames are used.

Summary

This chapter has covered ideas to help you build the fourth frame management skill: the wise use of frames for persuasion and negotiation. For both persuasion and negotiation, the results will be better to the extent that one can know one's frame and the frames of others.

Scan all change efforts and you find a poor performance average, something on the order of 50 percent. Successful change efforts are due, in part, to effective persuasion. Effective persuasion is achieved by shifting the decision frame of those being persuaded, enabling them to "see the light," to see what was hidden.

For persuasion, knowing the frame of the ones to be persuaded reveals the frame shift strategy for effective persuasion. For negotiation, as we have seen, knowing the other parties' frames is essential for crafting a successful outcome.

All of the concepts in Chapters 1-4 can be brought into use in shaping a successful approach to persuasion and negotiation. Try them the next time you must handle a persuasion or negotiation. This will build your skill and demonstrate the value of frame shifting in this context.

6

FRAME TRAPS

There is always an easy solution to every human problem -- neat, plausible, and wrong.

H. L. Mencken

Mental traps abound. They pop up everywhere. And they can frustrate you as you try to make a good decision. They can fool you into thinking you are viewing a situation correctly when you are not. They can fool you into thinking you are making good decisions when you are not. They can fool you into thinking a bad outcome is just bad luck when it is really the result of your own flawed thinking.

And they can fool you into thinking you are not caught in a trap when you are.

Your decisions *will* be better once you learn to detect and avoid these frame traps. This is the fifth frame management skill you need for better decisions.

There is a considerable body of research and literature on decision traps.[1] I will draw on this work and my own experience as we explore what to avoid. We will look first at five traps to watch for at all times. Then we will walk together through the steps of a decision, look at how to avoid the frame traps that can appear at each step, I will conclude with an examination of two process-related traps that prevent us from seeing other traps.

Watch Out for These!

The following five traps can arise in all aspects of decision making and lead to bad frames and bad decisions:

1. Trend following
2. Anchoring
3. Recency
4. Overconfidence
5. Cause-effect confusion

Let's see what these are and why they are dangerous.

1. Trend Following

This is the trap of thinking something will continue to keep going along as it has in the past. This trap was at work in 2005-6 when many people bought houses they could not afford. Their perceived gap was lack of a "suitable" house. They concluded the too-expensive house was a good choice to close the gap because they assumed housing prices would continue to go up. Over the next three years, housing prices declined dramatically, and many variable rate mortgages reset at higher monthly payments. The result was a wave of foreclosures, millions of unhappy people, and the subprime mortgage crisis of 2007-8 which crushed the housing industry for five years.

Avoid this trap. Check whether you think any trends important to a decision will continue. Analyze these trends. Identify what can bring them to a halt, reverse them, or speed them up. Use these findings to refine the trend assumptions.

2. Anchoring[2]

In making assumptions about numerical values, our minds are anchored by any initial estimates we encounter. Imagine it is 2005. You are told that the price of a gallon of gasoline in Los Angeles is $1.85 per gallon. You are asked to guess what the price will be in Los Angeles in eight years. Most people would guess at prices ranging from $1.50 to $2.50, a range close to, but slightly higher than, the $1.85 price. If so, they would have been anchored by the $1.85 price and by their knowledge of recent trends in gasoline prices. And they would have been wrong. Nine years later, the price of a gallon of gasoline had more than doubled, to around $4.00.

Here is another example. How many different ways can you arrange 10 books on a shelf? Make a quick guess before reading further.

Most people will begin thinking about arrangements and get anchored by the first guesses they make, ending up with estimates ranging from a few hundred to a few thousand ways. The correct answer is 3,628,800 ways!

The best way to deal with the Anchoring Trap is to start with two greatly different estimates for the quantity in question, not just one. That way you will be less likely to get trapped by an initial single estimate. This antidote works well for estimates like the gasoline price example, but not so well for estimates like the book-combinations example.

3. Recency[2]

Our assumptions can be overly influenced by recent information. In the extreme, this tendency can lead to manias such as the dot-com stock market bubble in 2000 and the housing mania of 2006. Protect yourself from this trap by looking at older information, as well as recent, to achieve a more balanced perspective.

4. Overconfidence[1]

Often, we are overconfident when asked to tell how much we do not know about something. To illustrate, here is a test for you. Three quantities are described in the table that follows.

For each of them, guess a low and high value. Make your estimates far enough apart so that, in each case, there is an 80 percent chance the actual value falls between them. Go ahead. Give it a try. Write down your estimates:

Quantity	Low Estimate	High Estimate
U.S. Population in 1900, millions		
Height of Mt. Everest, feet		
Price of gold on December 28, 2007, $/oz		

I will give you the answers in a moment, but first, let's talk about what you probably did. Most people make their ranges too narrow and only about half the actual values end up falling inside their ranges, not 80% of them as requested. People make the ranges too narrow because they are overconfident about the uncertainty of their knowledge. The reasons for this are not entirely clear.

I have found three ways to guard against this trap.

1. In estimating quantities, estimate a range, and keep widening the range until you feel silly about how wide it is. When you sense the silliness, you have probably got a range that reflects properly your lack of knowledge.

2. Do daily practice in estimating ranges around uncertain quantities that you can check, like tomorrow's temperature, future prices of commodities or securities, and the final scores from

sporting events. Each day, check how you did on the estimates from the prior day. When I do this practice, I find that my ranges are too narrow to begin with, but eventually I am able to estimate true 80-percent ranges. Do this practice and the resulting self-calibration will carry over into better estimates related to your decisions.

3. Assess how well your decision choice will hold up if a key quantity is significantly different from its assumed value. If the outcome is insensitive to the value, the Overconfidence Trap is not a problem. If the outcome is sensitive, the estimate of the key quantity needs to be checked carefully.

And now for the answers. The correct values for the three quantities are as follows: U.S. population in 1900 was 76.2 million people. Mount Everest is 29,035 feet high. The price of gold on December 31, 2007 was $840 per ounce.

How did you do? At least two of the three true values should have fallen between your lows and your highs. If none or only one did, you were caught in the Overconfidence Trap.

Organization leaders are snared by a variant of the Overconfidence Trap when their decisions are shaped by the following beliefs:

- Their estimates of time and cost are reasonable.
- They can accurately define the benefits of their decision choices.
- The current situation is sufficiently similar to a prior one to be guided by the prior situation.
- They have good decision-making skill, based on success with one or more prior, seemingly similar decisions.
- They can totally control implementing a decision.

Often not one of these beliefs is true. And they lead to frames that produce gullible, impetuous choices and bad results.

In the oil industry, the overconfidence in estimates is summed up in the term, "winner's curse." The term comes from competitive bidding on tracts of land for oil exploration. The winning bidders tend to lose. Why? Because the winners have the most optimistic estimates of exploration success and cost. On average, the actual exploration results are well below the optimistic estimates. To make matters worse, the optimistic failures cannot be offset by pessimistic success since pessimistic bids don't win any tracts for exploration.[3]

Overestimates of benefits and underestimates of cost and time routinely plague decisions made about major projects: change initiatives, new-product development projects, infrastructure projects, new software systems, new factories, integration of an acquired company, expansion into new regions. These bad estimates are due to the Overconfidence Trap.

The consequences of this trap are worse if there is overconfidence about decision-making skill and control of implementation..

Quaker Oats' acquisition of Snapple, described in Chapter 2, is an example of the harm caused by overconfidence about perceived situational similarity, decision-making skill, and implementation control. The Quaker Oats' executives were overly confident that Snapple was like Gatorade, that they knew how to make the right decisions about Snapple, and that they knew how to implement their Snapple strategy successfully. The result was a disaster.

Overcoming the varieties of the Overconfidence Trap just described is not easy. Two practices can help. First, declare that the trap exists and all assumptions based on estimates of future outcomes are suspect. Second, use rough probability distributions for cost and time estimates, rather than single-number estimates.

A few successes can breed overconfidence. Avoid this by probing those successes dispassionately. Were you good or were you just lucky? Assess what happened as expected and what occurred by chance that helped. Summarize first what was done poorly, then what was done well. In other words, do a debriefing and follow-up of successful decisions to understand exactly why you succeeded.

One final aspect of overconfidence: the belief that the decision outcome can be easily controlled. This belief leads to a bad decision frame about implementing new initiatives and to a consequent lack of adequate oversight and steering control. Then, as time goes on, the inertia of old ways and the occurrence of random surprises can combine to hobble and eventually halt the implementation.

5. Cause-Effect Confusion

In logic, this goes by the phrase "post hoc, ergo propter hoc:" if one thing appears after another, the first thing must have caused the second. This trap appears all the time in making decisions about processes that are not working well.

When a problem appears, people look at the immediately preceding steps in the process for the cause when, quite often, something more subtle is at work. Practices from improvement methodologies such as Six Sigma and Total Quality Management avoid this trap by focusing on root causes, rather than symptoms. Those practices should be adopted for any decision.

What Lurks at Each Step

In prior chapters, I described decision making using a simplified six step process. In this chapter, we will use a slightly more detailed eight-step process in order to expose the traps you need to consider. Let's begin by listing the eight steps:

1. Perceive an apparent gap--the gap between what you want and what you have initiates the impulse to make a decision.
2. Make assumptions about the gap--perception of a gap triggers thoughts about the nature of the gap, and what, if anything, you can do about it.
3. Decide about a decision--thinking about the gap

eventually leads you to a pre-decision as to whether or not you should do something to close the gap.

4. Pose the framing question--once you decide you want to do something to close the gap, you describe your task in the form of a question, such as "Where shall I go on vacation?" or "What shall I do on vacation?." As you now know, the choice of a good framing question is the most important factor for a good decision.

5. Make assumptions based on the framing question--as discussed in Chapter 2, the choice of the framing question will inevitably lead us to make assumptions about the situation. For example, with the "Where shall I go on vacation?" framing question, you assume location-related vacation attributes are more important. With the "What shall I do on vacation?" question, activity-related attributes are more important. The assumption about what is important always shifts when the question is changed.

6. Search for choices--identify possible ways to answer the framing question and thereby close the gap.

7. Select the best choice--you evaluate the choices identified and pick the best one.

8. Implement the choice--you plan how you will make the choice happen, then carry out your plan and thereby, hopefully, achieve success by closing the gap between the current situation and the state of affairs you want.

There are traps waiting to catch you at each step. Let's see what they are.

Step 1--Perceive the Gap

Watch out for two traps in this first step, the *Mirage Trap* and the *Denial Trap*. You fall into the Mirage Trap when you believe there is a gap, but one really doesn't exist. This trap may be at work, for example, when someone thinks a boy behaving in a normally energetic boyish way is not normal, but is instead, hyperactive and suffers from ADHD. To close the perceived, but false gap, between the boy's behavior and a desired norm, the lad is forced to take Ritalin or some similar pharmaceutical, and quite possibly ends up with unpleasant long-term consequences for his health.

The best way to avoid the Mirage Trap is to identify and confirm the assumptions on which the gap is based.

Many times, this will be sufficient to dissipate any mirages and avoid needless work and stress.

You are caught in the second trap, the Denial Trap, if you convince yourself that no gap exists when one really does. U.S. tire makers were caught in the Denial Trap in the 1960's and 70's.[4] For decades, they had done well by selling replacement tires. The top four companies were a highly regarded and profitable de-facto oligopoly, with Goodyear its largest member. The bias-ply tires they made lasted only about 14,000 miles, so car owners always needed tire replacements, which could be sold at high margins.

The U.S. tire companies knew about the steel-belted radial Michelin tire, first made in 1948, which could last over 40,000 miles. Here was a major threat, creating a gap between what the U.S. tire makers were doing versus what they needed to do to survive. Yet the companies denied the existence of the threat, denied the gap. The Michelin tire, they said, was all right for the European roads, but not the U.S. market.

U.S. sales of steel-belted radial tires rose rapidly and U.S. tire companies went into a decline that lasted several decades.

To avoid the Denial Trap, periodically identify possible threats and opportunities. Do a good job of assessing the likelihood of these possibilities.

Before dismissing a possible threat or opportunity, take a closer look at the reasons for dismissal. Confirm that the assumptions behind the dismissal are valid. If the reasons for dismissal are not valid, the threat or opportunity may be real. Recognizing the threat or opportunity is real leads to recognition of a gap.

Having successfully avoided the Mirage and Denial Traps, let's move on to the next step of our journey to a decision.

Step 2 -- Make Assumptions about the Gap

When you think about a perceived gap, you make a number of assumptions. The five common traps described at the start of the chapter can trick you into thinking you are making good assumptions about the gap when you are making bad ones. So, watch out for them at this Step and

throughout the decision process. When you spot one, take
the appropriate corrective action to eliminate the trap.

Step 3 -- Decide about the Decision

You are vulnerable to two traps when you think
about whether or not to make a decision in response to a
perceived gap. These are the *False Urgency* and *Pain-
Avoidance Traps*.

The False Urgency Trap causes you to believe you
must take action, and soon, when delay really is
acceptable, and may even be beneficial if the additional
time leads to a better decision. Sales people frequently
use the False Urgency Trap to induce a customer to make
a purchase. Counteract this trap by thinking through the
pluses and minuses of delay.

The Pain Avoidance Trap can catch you when you
confront a difficult, highly emotional decision. To avoid the
pain of the decision, you may procrastinate until
circumstances compel you to act.   The U.S. tire
manufacturers mentioned earlier were caught in this trap,
as well as the Denial Trap. Many firms faced with the need
to act to counteract competitive threats have been
hampered by this trap.

Another area that can spring the Pain Avoidance Trap is decisions on personnel issues. Many managers, for example, will put off doing reviews of their direct reports for this reason, resulting in poor communication and continued poor performance.

Avoid the Pain Avoidance Trap. First check to see if it is present and causing procrastination. If so, then acknowledge the procrastination and shift your perspective. You are, after all, seeking to improve a situation, close a gap. If the improvement will make a big difference, you and the people that matter to you will be better off once you have acted.

Think also about the price you are paying personally and in terms of organization performance by not acting.

Step 4 -- Pose the Framing Question

Myopia is a trap you can fall into when you choose the framing question. Suppose you are dealing with a situation in which a worker is not processing customer requests fast enough. How would you pose the framing question?

It might be "Why can't the worker do better?" But notice how this question focuses on the worker and not the process of which the worker is a part. The question is too narrow in its focus, too myopic in the range of improvement possibilities it leads to. A better question would be "How can we improve the process of which the worker is part?"

This opens up a much better range of possibilities. In general, in organizational situations, it is always better to use a framing question that focuses on the entire system involved, rather than just on the local symptoms. This is, of course, one of the key ideas from Six Sigma, Total Quality Management, and business process reengineering.

The last parts of Chapter 4 provide suggestions for choosing a good framing question.

Step 5 -- Make Assumptions

Once you have chosen your framing question, it leads to other assumptions about the situation. As you make these assumptions, you are again vulnerable to the five traps described earlier in connection with gap assumptions.

In addition, watch out for the *Confirmation Bias Trap*. This is the tendency to seek only information that confirms a belief, and not information that disproves the belief. This trap was at work at General Motors in the 1970's when it dismissed the Japanese threat, at Kmart in the 1980's when it dismissed the Walmart threat, and at Blockbuster in the 2000's when it initially dismissed the seriousness of the Netflix threat.

You can avoid the Confirmation Bias Trap by first identifying the beliefs that might be affected by it and then deliberately seeking to disprove those assumptions. Challenge the sacred cows!

Step 6 -- Search for Choices

Once a decision is defined by its framing question, the search for choices begins. The search can be hampered by the *Quick-Grab* and *Hamlet Traps*.

You are caught by the *Quick-Grab Trap* when you identify just one or two answers to the framing question, grab one of them and act on it. The Quick-Grab is another variation of "act in haste, repent forever." We are particularly vulnerable to this trap if emotions are high or we are tired when seeking to make a decision.

Avoid the Quick-Grab Trap by forcing yourself to come up with a larger number of choices, say at least 6-8, and then rating those choices against appropriate criteria. Just going through those steps will slow you down and give you a better decision. If you are too tired to come up with choices, don't fall into the False Urgency Trap. Delay things until you have more energy to come up with a good range of choices.

The *Hamlet Trap* is named after the lead character in Shakespeare's play *Hamlet* who endlessly ponders decision alternatives until events overtake him and lead to him to a tragic end. As noted in Chapter 3, people without emotion are always caught in this Trap. They can never make a final choice, but must continue to endlessly evaluate the alternatives.

If you have been involved with a decision having several choices that has been studied for some time, chances are you are in the Hamlet Trap. Get out of the trap by setting a time limit for making the decision or dropping it. Before the deadline, list the options you have and pick the best of them. Then compare the consequences of doing nothing or doing the best option. If the consequences, feel equally favorable, just toss a coin and go with the outcome of the toss. But get out of the trap. It is debilitating and demoralizing.

Step 7 -- Select the Best Choice

Two traps to watch for in making your choice are ones mentioned earlier--Myopia and Confirmation Bias. A third trap arises in selecting a choice. It is the *Sunk-Cost*

Trap.[5]

This is the favoring of one choice because so much has already been invested in it. That investment may be lost if the choice is rejected, and the social cost of rejecting the choice may be high.

To avoid these three traps, explore a wide-enough range of choices. That way you are unlikely to overlook one that is very different, but with the potential to be very effective. Do not consider just ideas you are initially comfortable and familiar with. In rating possible choices, do not bias your ratings in favor of ones you are leaning toward unless you have good evidence that those ratings will stand up to scrutiny.

When a group is making a choice, avoid the traps by using a good process to identify and evaluate choices. The process must be designed so the group considers a wide range of choices and engages in constructive dissent to select the best choice.

Step 8 -- Implement the Choice

Once you have made a decision and begin to implement it, you are exposed to two more traps, the *Tedium Trap* and the *False Completion Trap*. The making of a decision, particularly a key strategic decision about an organization, can be an emotionally charged activity that gets everyone up to a high energy level. In contrast, the actual implementation of the decision can feel like the day after a great party. You now actually have to do something and it won't be glamorous.

Nor will you be a hero right away by doing the implementing.

You will be tempted to get to the implementation only after you attend to 'more important" daily fire fights. This is the Tedium Trap kicking in. Big mistake. A new decision is something newborn and without sufficient early nurturing, it will die.

Avoid the Tedium Trap by establishing and using a disciplined process to plan and carry out the implementation of the decision, including periodic meetings (even if they are just with yourself) to assess progress.

The False-Completion Trap is the premature declaration that the implementation is done and successful. It appears often in two settings: software implementation and integration of a new acquisition. Executives sponsoring software projects can be fooled into believing the new software implementation is done once any new equipment needed is in place, the software is installed, and people are trained in its use. In fact, all of that represents just the first third of the implementation. If the sponsoring executive moves on too soon because of the False-Completion Trap, chances are the new software won't be fully or properly utilized, and the expected performance gains won't happen. In the worst cases, the implementation failure can and has killed organizations.

The same problems arise when one company acquires another and begins the process of assimilation. Without proper attention to differences in systems and cultures, the assimilation won't happen and the acquiring company will get a poor return on its acquisition investment.

To avoid the False Completion Trap with an acquisition, define ahead of time a set of performance measures that must be achieved before successful integration can be declared, then track progress against those measures. Do not declare victory until the measures have been achieved.

Process Traps

We have just exposed fifteen traps that can snare you when making a decision. You may not even be aware of it when one of these traps has caught you, particularly if you are also caught by a process trap.

Two process traps to avoid: *Bias for Action Trap* and the *Mindlessness Trap*.

People get snared in the Bias-for-Action Trap by their impatience. They feel it is a waste of time to ponder the frame they are using for a decision. "Of course it's the right way to describe the decision," they say. "Let's get on with it and decide what to do." But by now, you know better. If the frame is bad, the hasty person is in trouble.

As noted earlier, making a decision is analogous to developing a new product or service. Your success rate goes up if you spend enough time at the start thinking through the development plan and specifications. And at the start, you can make changes most easily and cheaply.

What is true for product development, is true for decisions. Spend sufficient time at the start of any important decision to make sure the frame is good. Don't rush on to other steps of the decision until the frame is right.

As noted earlier, the bias-for-action trap also hurts decision making by limiting choices considered. Impatience curtails the search for options, favoring the first "good" choice found and acting on it. Even worse, the criteria for favoring the choice are not defined well, nor are they validated.

No one wants paralysis by analysis. That's how battles are lost. But *some* time spent finding a good frame and a large enough range of choices will increase potential for success.

The Mindlessness Trap, a frequent companion of the Bias-for-Action Trap, is at work when people go through the steps of a decision without thinking about them, paying little attention to the assumptions being made, the framing question being used, and the true quality of the choices being made.[6] This trap arises when your organization or person has used the same procedures too long without any change.

The antidote is to schedule a day every six months or so to review how key decisions were made and check for presence of the Mindlessness Trap.

Death Spiral

When traps lead to bad frames, and bad frames lead to bad results, efforts to improve are hampered by still more traps:

- Hasty action, a common response to crises from bad decisions,
- Too myopic and narrow a search for better frames and better choices,
- Defensiveness and associated negative reactions to helpful suggestions,
- Stubborn adherence to a bad course of action because of sunk costs,
- Failure to admit failure because of personal or corporate political and emotional reasons,
- Culture-induced resistance to exploration of options,

As I described in Chapter 3, the intense emotions arising from the results of bad decisions breed more traps like the ones just described. If such traps are not detected and avoided, one bad frame can lead to a worse one in a downward spiral of bad decisions and bad outcomes – a self-reinforcing feedback loop with potentially lethal results for an organization or an individual.

Summary

You now are aware of the subtle frame traps ready to snare you. Exhibit 6.1 lists the traps you may encounter. Think through your last few major decisions. Assess the extent to which any of the traps was present.

Do a post-decision assessment of traps on a regular basis. Were you caught by any? Did they hurt the decision quality? As you keep doing this, your decisions will get better and better.

Exhibit 6.1 -- Full List of Frame Traps Described in Chapter 6

Decision Step	Frame Traps to Avoid
All decision steps	Trend Following, Anchoring, Recency, Overconfidence, Cause-Effect Confusion
Perceive an apparent gap.	Mirage, Denial
Make assumptions about the gap.	Trend Following, Anchoring, Recency, Overconfidence, Cause-Effect Confusion
Decide about a decision.	False Urgency, Pain Avoidance
Pose the framing question.	Myopia
Make assumptions based on the framing question.	Trend Following, Anchoring, Recency, Overconfidence, Cause-Effect Confusion, Confirmation Bias
Search for choices.	Quick Grab, Hamlet
Select the best choice.	Myopia, Confirmation Bias, Sunk Cost
Implement the choice.	Overconfidence, Tedium, False Completion
Process Traps	Bias for Action, Mindlessness

BETTER DECISIONS

You now know about the five frame-management skills that lead you to better decisions:

1. Frame awareness (Chapters 1 and 2),
2. Management of emotions (Chapter 3),
3. Frame shift skill (Chapter 4),
4. Frames to persuade and negotiate (Chapter 5),
5. Avoidance of frame traps (Chapter 6).

Practice the suggestions for improving these skills and check periodically on how you are doing. To improve these skills usually requires breaking old habits. That can only be done through repetition and periodic assessment, but it can be done. And any degree of improvement will mean better decisions.

Start today trying out the ideas I have provided. As you make decisions during the day, pause to consider how you make them. Notice how you frame them. Were the frames good ones? Did you actually start with one frame then shift to a better one? Did you avoid any of the traps described in Chapter 6? Did you draw on the concepts in Chapter 5 in any attempts to persuade or negotiate? Did you notice the impact of your emotions on the quality of your decisions?

At the end of each day, review the quality of your decisions and grade the results. Also, assess how you did in using the five key skills. The more you do this, the better your decisions will be.

If you would like to share with me your experiences in using the ideas in this book, please do so. It is always helpful to learn about the success people enjoy with good frames. Use lynndavidson@directionfocus.com to reach me.

For decisions to be made in meetings, use a meeting design that leads to good decision frames. Suggestions for how to design successful meetings can be found in my eBook *Meeting Power*, which is available from Amazon.

Best wishes for success with your decisions.

NOTES

Chapter 1

1. See, for example, Howard Raffia: *Decision Analysis: Introductory Lectures on Choices under Uncertainty*. Reading, Ma.: Addison-Wesley. 1968; Herbert A. Simon: *The New Science of Management Decisions*, rev ed. Englewood Cliffs, N.J. Prentice Hall. 1977; J. Edward Russo and Paul J. H. Schoemaker: *Winning Decisions: Getting it Right the First Time.* New York: Currency Doubleday. 2002; John S. Hammond, Ralph L. Keeney and Howard Raiffa: *Smart Choices: A Practical Guide to Making Better Decisions.* New York: Broadway Books. 2002.; David Henderson: *Making Great Decisions in Business and* Life (Chicago: Chicago Park Press, 2005); and Jonah Lehrer: *How We Decide* (Mariner Books, 2010).
2. J. Edward Russo and Paul J. H. Schoemaker: *Decision Traps: The Ten Barriers to Brilliant Decision-Making & How to Overcome* Them. New York: Doubleday. 1989. Chapter 2. Also *Winning Decisions: Getting it Right the First Time.* New York: Currency Doubleday. 2002. Chapters 2 and 3.
3. Chip Heath and Dan Heath: *Decisive: Hot to Make Better Choices in Life and Work.* New York: Crown Books. 2013.
4. For a good account of the history of General Motors' decline read "A giant falls: The collapse of General Motors into bankruptcy is only the latest chapter in a long story of mismanagement and decline," *The Economist* (June 4, 2009).

5. Daniel Quinn Mills and G. Bruce Friesen: *Broken Promises: An Unconventional View of What Went Wrong at IBM.* Boston: Harvard Business Review Press. 1996.
6. Herbert A. Simon: *The New Science of Management Decisions*, rev ed. Englewood Cliffs, N.J.: Prentice Hall. 1977.
7. Henry Ford: *My Life and Work.* CreateSpace, 2011.
8. Gary A. Klein: *Sources of Power: How People Make Decisions.* Cambridge: The MIT Press.1999.
9. Robert B. Cialdini: *Influence: The Psychology of Persuasion.* New York: HarperCollins. 2000. Chapter 1.
10. Hernán Cortés de Monroy y Pizarro made an irreversible decision in July 1519 in Mexico when he sank his ships leaving his men with no choice but to fight the Aztecs and ultimately conquer Mexico. Wikipedia has a good description of the almost unbelievable saga of Hernando Cortés's conquest of Mexico. For a detailed account, see also Hugh Thomas: *Conquest: Cortes, Montezuma, and the Fall of Old Mexico.* New York: Simon & Schuster. 1995.
11. Gary A. Klein: *Sources of Power: How People Make Decisions.* Cambridge: The MIT Press. 1999.
12. Jim Collins: *Good to Great.* New York: Harper Business. 2001. Appendix 1A.

Chapter 2

1. Information on the Snapple case had been drawn from the following sources: Sidney Finkelstein: *Why Smart Executives Fail.* London: Penguin Books. 2003. 77-83; Greg Burns:"Crunch Time at Quaker

Oats," *Business Week,* 26 September 1996, 70;
Greg Burns: "What Price the Snapple Debacle?,"
Business Week, 14 April, 1997, 42; Nikhil Deagun:
"Triarc Revives Snapple's Wendy," *The Wall Street
Journal,* 6 June 1997; John Deighton: "How a Juicy
Brand Came Back to Life," *Harvard Business
School Week,* 4 April, 2002, available at
http://hbswk.hbs.edu/item/2752.html; Darren
Rovell: "Interview with Bill Smithburg, Former
Quaker Chairman and CEO," available at
http://firstinthirst.typepad.com/darren_rovells_blog_
on_al/2005/11/interview_with_.html.
The Snapple purchase has been fodder for many
business school lectures and case studies. I
believe the case studies focused on the strategy
issues related to the success of Snapple, with less
emphasis given to the decision process Quaker
Oats used.

Chapter 3

1. See the following for evidence that people without
   emotion have trouble making decisions: Antonio R.
   Damasio: *Descartes' Error: Emotion, Reason, and
   the Human Brain.* New York: Grosset/Putnam.
   1994; James Notrier: "Emotion, Neuroscience, and
   Investing: Investors as Dopamine Addicts," *Global
   Equity Strategies.* January 20, 2005; Antoine
   Bechara: "The Role of Emotion in Decision-making:
   Evidence from Neurological Patients with
   Orbitofrontal Damage," *Brain and Cognition 55.*
   2004. Pp. 30-40.

2. *David Voreacos and David Glovin,* "Madoff
   Confessed $50 Billion Fraud Before FBI   Arrest
   (Update3)," *Bloomberg News,*December   12,
   2008. Diana B.Henriques, "   Madoff   is

Sentenced to 150 Years for Ponzi Scheme," *New York Times,* June 29, 2009.

3. Christopher J. Anderson "The functions of emotion in decision making and decision avoidance," in Kathleen D. Vohs, Ray F. Baumestier, and George Lowenstein, eds.: *Do Emotions Help or Hurt Decision Making: Hedgefoxian Perspective*, Russell Sage Foundation, 2007.

4. Bethany McLean and Peter Elkind: *The Smartest Guys in the Room:The Amazing Rise and Scandalous Fall of Enron.* Portfolio Trade. 2004.

5. For further discussion and references on the issue of CEO pride in acquisitions see: Chip Heath and Dan Heath: *Decisive: How to Make Better Choices in Life and* Work, New York: Crown Business. 2013.

6. Robert Barker, "Newell Rubbermaid: Why It'll Bounce Back," *Business Week* (October 20, 2003) 164.

7. Peter F. Drucker: *Management: Tasks, Responsibilities, Practices* New York: Harper& Row, 1974. 472.

8. Del Jones, "When You're Smiling Are You Seething Inside": *U.S.A. Today*, April 12, 2004.

Chapter 4

1. James Damore: "Why I Was Fired by Google," *The Wall Street Journal,* August 11, 2017.

2. Sydney Finkelstein: *Why Smart Executives Fail.* London: Penguin Books. 2003.

3. Richard Foster: *Innovation: The Attacker's Advantage.* New York: Summit Books. 1986. p 139.

4. Jeffrey M. Schwartz, M.D. and Sharon Begley: *The Mind and the Brain: Neuroplasticity and the Power*

of *Mental Force*. New York: Harper Collins. 2002; Nicholas Carr, in Chapter 2 of *The Shallows: What the Internet is Doing to Our Brains*. New York: Norton. 2011. Provides a good description of the paradigm shift from the belief in a fixed structure of the mature mind to the belief that the mind constantly changes. See also the Wikipedia entry on neuroplasticity.

5. For a good history of Howard Johnson's success with frame shifting see the following Website page: http://www.hojoland.com/history.html.

6. James Collins: *Good to Great*. New York: Harper Business. 2001. Ch 1.

7. James Collins: ibid Ch. 2.

8. Andrew Grove: *Only the Paranoid* Survive. New York. Currency Doubleday. 1996. Pages 81-93. Chip Heath and Dan Heath: *Decisive: How to Make Better Choices in Life and Work*. New York: Crown Business. 2013, Pages 12-15

9. "Reshaping Cisco: The world according to Chambers" *The Economist*. August 27, 2009.

10. For additional ideas on how to shift to a better frame see pages 45-48 of J. Edward Russo and Paul J.H. Schoemaker, *Winning Decisions*, New York: Doubleday. 2002.

Chapter 5

1. For ideas on persuasion see the following: Robert B. Cialdini: *Influence: The Psychology of* Persuasion. New York: Collins Business. 1984; and Kerry Patterson et al: *Influencer: The Power to Change* Anything. New York: McGraw-Hill. Chapter 1 of Cialdini's book includes a discussion of how the click-whirr response pattern people (and other animals) exhibit can be an effective tool of

negotiation. The person agreeing to something is not aware of why he or she is agreeing. It is like a conditioned reflex. For ideas on negotiation, see the following: Roger Fisher, William L. Urey, and Bruce Patton: *Getting to Yes: Negotiating Agreement without Giving In.* New York: Penguin Books. 2011; and Roy Lewicki, David Saunders, and Bruce Barry: *Negotiation.* New York: McGraw-Hill. 2009. For ideas on shifting someone else's frame see J. Edward Russo and Paul J. H. Schoemaker: *Winning Decisions.* New York: Doubleday. 2002. Pp 49-50.

2. Gordon Bethune: *From Worst to First: Behind the Scenes of Continental's Remarkable Comeback.* New York: Wiley. 1998.

3. See Wikipedia entry "Southern California Supermarket Strike of 2003-4" at http://en.wikipedia.org/wiki/Southern_California_Sup ermarket_strike_of_2003-2004

Chapter 6

1. Amos Tversky and Daniel Kahneman conducted extensive research on frame traps and published some of the seminal research on the subject. Their landmark paper, "Judgment under uncertainty: Heuristics and biases," *Science,* 1974, *185,* 1124-1131 is highly recommended. See also the following: Daniel Kahneman, Paul Slovic, and Amos Taversky: *Judgment under uncertainty: Heuristics and biases.* Cambridge University Press, 1982. This book contains their 1974 paper and many other articles on frame traps. For more recent works on frame traps, see the following: J. Edward Russo and Paul J.H. Schoemaker: *Decision Traps.,* New York: Doubleday. 1989; Gary Belsky and Thomas Gilovich: *Why Smart*

People Make Big Money Mistakes. New York: Simon & Schuster. 1999; Scott Plous: *The Psychology of Judgment and Decision Making*. New York: McGraw-Hill, 1993.

2. For more on the anchoring and recency traps, see the Tversky and Kahneman 1974 *Science* article referenced in 1 above and also pp.85-92 of the Russo and Schoemaker book in 1 above.

3. The first published analysis of The Winner's Curse Trap was an article by three engineers at Atlantic Richfield, Ed Capen, Robert Clapp, and William Campbell. See "Competitive Bidding in High-Risk Situations," *Journal of Petroleum Technology, 23*, June 1971, 641-53.

4. Richard S. Tedlow and David Ruben: "The Dangers of Wishful Thinking," *Harvard Business Review*, Jan-Feb 2008.

5. The sunk cost trap has been examined by many social psychologists and economists. Many interesting studies are listed on Wikipedia. See, for example, Hal Arkes and Catherine Blumer: "The Psychology of Sunk Cost". *Organizational Behavior and Human Decision Process, 35*. 1985. 124–140.

6. For a good and entertaining discussion of mindlessness and how it can trip you up, see Ellen J. Sanger: *Mindfulness*. Addison-Wesley. 1989.

INDEX

ABOUT THE AUTHOR

Lynn B. Davidson helps corporations and non-profit organizations achieve success in achieving their visions. His support includes the design and facilitation of vision and growth strategy sessions that use frame shifts to find superior ideas and make successful decisions.

He also shares ideas on strategy success and good decisions through presentations, publications, and *The Competitive Edge* newsletter, available to executives upon request.

Lynn started his consulting practice, after a successful career in the oil industry, first in research, then as a strategic planning executive with Getty Oil Company. He holds BS, MS, and PhD degrees in engineering from Stanford University.

Made in the USA
San Bernardino, CA
28 March 2019